Developing a
LEARNING
CLASSROOM

Developing a
LEARNING
CLASSROOM

Moving Beyond Management Through *Relationships, Relevance,* and *Rigor*

Nic Cooper
Betty K. Garner

CORWIN
A SAGE Company

CORWIN
A SAGE Company

FOR INFORMATION:

Corwin
A SAGE Company
2455 Teller Road
Thousand Oaks, California 91320
(800) 233-9936
www.corwin.com

SAGE Publications Ltd.
1 Oliver's Yard
55 City Road
London, EC1Y 1SP
United Kingdom

SAGE Publications India Pvt. Ltd.
B 1/I 1 Mohan Cooperative Industrial Area
Mathura Road, New Delhi
India 110 044

SAGE Publications Asia-Pacific Pte. Ltd.
3 Church Street
#10-04 Samsung Hub
Singapore 049483

Acquisitions Editor: Jessica Allan
Associate Editor: Allison Scott
Editorial Assistant: Lisa Whitney
Permissions Editor: Karen Ehrmann
Project Editor: Veronica Stapleton
Copy Editor: Lana Todorovic-Arndt
Typesetter: Hurix Systems Pvt. Ltd.
Proofreader: Gretchen Treadwell
Indexer: Gloria Tierney
Cover Designer: Karine Hovsepian

Printed in the United States of America

Library of Congress Cataloging-in-Publication Data

Cooper, Nic, author.

Developing a learning classroom : moving beyond management through relationships, relevance, and rigor / Nic A. Cooper, Betty K. Garner.

pages cm

Includes bibliographical references and index.

ISBN 978-1-4522-0388-1 (pbk. : alk. paper)

1. Classroom environment. 2. Teacher-student relationships. I. Garner, Betty K., author. II. Title.

LB3013.C5655 2012

371.102′4—dc23

2012012486

This book is printed on acid-free paper.

12 13 14 15 16 10 9 8 7 6 5 4 3 2 1

Contents

Acknowledgments

Special thanks to Corwin for the opportunity for us to collaborate and share our combined knowledge and experience with teachers. We are grateful for the work of our editors, Jessica Allan and Lana Arndt, the Corwin production team, and the insightful feedback from the Corwin reviewers and colleagues who helped us refine the manuscript. Some of our colleagues who offered valuable feedback and encouragement are Cindy Buehler, Craig Gilroy, Sheila Chapman, Blaine Goodrich, and Dr. Patty Kaufman. We also extend special thanks to all the students, parents, and educators we have worked with, who have enriched our understanding of what it means to develop an effective learning classroom. The late Earnie Larsen, a mentor to Nic earlier in his career, and his work formed a basis for our perspective on the need to understand family of origin to understand oneself.

Betty also thanks her wonderful husband, Dr. John VanDruff, who provided love and encouragement throughout the writing process, even though he was dealing with chemotherapy for brain cancer. Jane, Nic's wife, has been a rock throughout his career and a constant source of strength and insight. Her support and patience have been a critical factor throughout this process.

PUBLISHER'S ACKNOWLEDGMENTS

Corwin wishes to acknowledge the following peer reviewers for their editorial insight and guidance.

Jeanne Marie Benoit
Seventh-Grade Teacher,
American History and
Language Arts
Putnam Middle School
Putnam, CT

Jamie Blassingame
Licensed Specialist in School
Psychology
Pearland ISD, Special Programs
Pearland, TX

Julie Duford
Fifth-Grade Teacher
Polson Middle School
Polson, MT

Kathy Ferrell
Instructional Coach
Excelsior Springs Middle School
Excelsior Springs, MO

Nicole Guyon
Resource Teacher
Community Preparatory School
Providence, RI

Susan Harmon
Technology Teacher
Neodesha Junior/Senior High
School
Neodesha, KS

Barb Keating
Educational Consultant, Retired
Principal
New Westminster, BC, Canada

Katina Keener
Assistant Principal
Peasley Middle School
Gloucester, VA

Alexis Ludewig
ABE Adjunct Instructor
Fox Valley Technical College
Appleton, WI

Sherry Markel
Professor
Northern Arizona University
College of Education,
Department of Teaching and
Learning
Flagstaff, AZ

John Pieper
Fifth-Grade Teacher, Read
School
Oshkosh Area School District
Oshkosh, WI

Ronda Schelvan
Autism Consultant and Special
Education Teacher
Washougal School District
Washougal, WA

Debbie Smith
Math Coach
Lady's Island Elementary
School
Beaufort, SC

Diane P. Smith
School Counselor
Smethport Area School District
Smethport, PA

Leslie Standerfer
Principal
Estrella Foothills High School
Goodyear, AZ

About the Authors

Nic Cooper, EdD, LPC, LMSW, has thirty-four years of experience in public education as a counselor, alternative education developer, assistant principal, and principal. He spent most of his career at the middle level after beginning as a high school counselor. Prior to his retirement, his middle school was named as one of Michigan's first Schools to Watch in 2006. He also has worked as a substance abuse counselor and a probation officer. After his retirement from public education, he has become a full-time faculty member in the teacher education program at Baker College in Jackson, MI and a part-time leadership coach for the Center for Excellence in Education at Central Michigan University. A certified counselor and social worker, Nic also works part-time as a therapist at Still Waters Counseling in Saline, MI. He is the state director for the Schools to Watch program, a recognition program for exemplary middle schools presented through the National Forum to Accelerate Middle Grades Reform. With Rick McCoy, he is the coauthor of a book for parents of adolescents titled *How to Keep Being a Parent When Your Child Stops Being a Child.* Nic is a member of the boards for the Michigan Association of Middle School Educators and the Michigan Association of Teacher Educators, as well as a member of the National Forum to Accelerate Middle Grades Reform. He presents at state and national conferences on classroom development, healing teaching staffs in conflict, and addressing the needs of at-risk students, among other topics.

Betty K. Garner, EdD, president of Aesthetic of Lifelong Learning, Inc., is dedicated to helping teachers, parents, and students develop their metability—the interactive dynamic of learning, creating, and changing. In over forty years as an educator, she has served as a classroom teacher, art teacher, psychological examiner, professional learning coach, university instructor, cognitive researcher, and international educational consultant. She has been involved in numerous privately and publicly funded innovative professional development projects that focused on developing learning communities, training teachers in action research, and facilitating teachers' portfolio preparation for National Board Certification. She continues to conduct seminars on her research throughout the United States and Europe. She is author of the popular book *Getting to "Got It!": Helping Struggling Students Learn How to Learn*, which gives teachers tools to help students develop their cognitive structures to more effectively gather, organize, and process information.

1

What Is a Learning Classroom?

How to Develop Relationships, Relevance, and Rigor

"It is the supreme art of the teacher to awaken joy in creative expression and knowledge."

—*Albert Einstein*

Jerry, an eager preservice teacher, was starting a class on behavior management before student teaching. In previous classes, he learned instructional theory and strategies. However, he continued to have nagging worries. Would his students listen to him? Would they behave? What if they didn't? Would he be able to relate to them? Would he have control and good classroom management? These fears preoccupied him. He didn't want anyone to know he felt this way.

Megan, Jerry's classmate, had similar concerns. She struggled with a perceived conflict between being nice and being tough. How would students enjoy her class if she must be firm to gain their respect? How would they like her if she had to consistently enforce school rules? She pretended to be confident.

When Megan and Jerry first walked into the class, they were surprised to find names on assigned seats. Class rules, which clearly stated expectations and criteria for failure, were projected on a screen. Dr. Roy Nickelson, the instructor, marched sternly into the class, stood at the podium, and in a stern voice stated, "This class is *the* most important class for teachers. If you are going to make it in this class, you have to work hard and follow my instructions on how to manage and control a classroom. You need to be prepared and to keep my rules. If you don't, you can't be a good teacher."

Students sat there, eyes glued on the rigid figure. He continued, "Now you have an idea of what expectations are for this class. Take a notebook and write your thoughts on classroom management and being in this class." The students dutifully followed directions.

After about three minutes, Dr. Roy changed his tone and politely asked students to move their chairs into a circle. He moved the podium to a corner and pulled his chair into the circle. In a gentle tone of voice, he invited students to take a deep breath and reflect on what just happened. There was a noticeable sigh of relief. Students responded to his invitation to share their thoughts and feelings about what they just experienced.

One student said, "At first, I felt the class was structured and efficient." Like many preservice teachers, this young man had learned that getting a good grade meant doing what he was told and giving the teacher what he or she wanted. Another said, "I thought, 'This is scary! I already hate this class!'" This student responded negatively and would typically choose to withdraw before it was too late. Some students, who had Dr. Roy for other classes, said they were really confused and wondered what happened to the other Dr. Roy, because this was so out of character for him.

Dr. Roy carefully planned this brief demonstration to help his students experience how students feel when they walk into a controlled, sterile, uninviting, oppressive, strictly managed classroom environment. Although the dramatization was difficult for Dr. Roy, he knew it was an effective tool to help his students become aware of how important it is to develop a learning classroom.

After the brief shock demo, Dr. Roy encouraged students to reflect on their feelings in a relaxed environment. In the circle, they felt more comfortable to share their ideas in an atmosphere of respect and acceptance. In response to their comments, Dr. Roy modeled active listening by paraphrasing to clarify rather than evaluating or lecturing. He used open-ended questions to stimulate discussion as they created meaning through collaboration.

When Dr. Roy joined his students in a circle, he focused on building relationships within a safe learning community. Such an environment usually prevents inappropriate behavior and learning happens fluidly and powerfully.

Fortunately for Jerry and Megan, they were participating in a class where the instructor developed a learning community and encouraged the participants to voice their thoughts and concerns. In this environment, students felt safe to be honest about their insecurities. This instructor actually modeled the difference between developing and managing a classroom in a way that was very different from the typical educational lecture classes where they were told how to teach content rather than shown how to engage learners. Dr. Roy emphasized, "You can manage a classroom with fear, but that discourages creative learning." He did not discard the need for managing or organizing the classroom. Instead, he emphasized the importance of focusing on interactive learning within a well-ordered, developed classroom.

When teacher education students in Dr. Roy's classroom management course were asked to think about how it would feel to develop a learning classroom rather than manage one, without exception, they were enthusiastic about developing one because it removed a substantial amount of the fear. One student said the change in terms changed his mental picture from "battening down the hatches" to "building something strong." It clearly represented a change in mindset.

Preservice teachers are confused and somewhat intimidated by the prospect of managing a classroom. This perspective permeates required courses like classroom management or behavior management. Teachers need to be effective and efficient; however, the word *manage* conveys a need to overpower or control. This often exacerbates their fears.

As noted earlier, it's not just the young teachers who struggle with this idea of managing a classroom. Seasoned teachers often believe they need to instill a certain fear in their students in order to keep them under control. This produces the illusion of a well-managed classroom. A well-managed classroom, though, is not necessarily one that promotes learning.

Even well-meaning teachers sometimes confuse managing and controlling the classroom with developing a learning classroom. Order in a classroom doesn't mean quiet; it means focused engagement where students understand the goals and feel safe getting involved. *It means focusing on relationships, relevance, and rigor.*

> Students tend to listen more with their hearts than with their heads.

THE THREE *R*s REVISITED

To effectively teach and awaken the joy that Einstein described, we need to focus on what matters—*relationships, relevance, rigor.* These three words appear frequently in educational journals and are often used in discussions about improving our schools. However, they are usually ordered differently: rigor, relevance, and relationships. Our decision to present these in reverse order is intentional, based on the primary importance of forming relationships to facilitate learning and the need for seeing relevance before looking deeper for rigor. We encourage teachers, both beginning and experienced, to recognize the importance of these three *R*s in developing a learning community within the classroom. We can become so busy just keeping up with everyday demands and managing details that we get caught in a survival mentality rather than enjoying and stimulating learning for ourselves and our students. In this book, we discuss many facets of effective teaching and learning that challenge our readers to take a different perspective on what matters.

From our years of experience, we realized that students tend to listen more with their hearts than with their heads. This insight opened our minds to carefully examine the effect of relationships on learning. Thousands of struggling students who turned their lives around reported that a caring teacher who believed in them made it possible for them to be successful. Good students who regularly got good grades reported that connecting with a caring teacher enabled them to excel in developing their abilities. At every age level, trusting relationships between teachers and students prime the brain for learning, activate willingness to cooperate, and encourage excellence.

Teachers who connect with their students create a safe environment where students can question, explore, and discover. Willingness to take risks can be limited by a fear of failure. A safe environment governed by principles that encourage growth and respect allows students the freedom to learn from their mistakes.

But what happens when teachers are uncomfortable building relationships with students? Teachers need to connect with kindness while maintaining appropriate boundaries. To build meaningful relationships, teachers need to know who they are, know their students, be competent in their content area, and be proficient in their ability to engage students in learning.

Students, who sometimes appear to resist learning, confront teachers by asking "Why do we need to know this?" This is a legitimate question. Instead of thinking students are just trying to avoid work, teachers need to look at the relevance of what they are teaching and how they are presenting it. Digital access to unlimited knowledge redefines the role of educators. As facilitators, teachers help equip students with the cognitive tools to learn, create, and change, so they can apply what they are learning to their own lives. With information doubling at astounding rates, teachers make instruction relevant by developing a learning community where students use rigorous, systematic approaches to build on the basics and enhance their cognitive capabilities to make sense of their changing world.

Although the term *rigor* usually connotes harsh inflexibility, we are using it to mean thoroughness and precise accuracy that is only possible with standards of excellence. A well-developed learning community provides the structure, opportunities, and security that challenge students to achieve depth and breadth of learning through self-discipline and continuing independent research. Rigor includes good organization and effective procedures that prevent many of the distracting behaviors interfering with learning.

As we worked with prospective and practicing teachers over the last three decades, we saw a need to emphasize the importance of developing a learning classroom based on relationships, relevance, and rigor, instead of stressing strategies for classroom and behavior management. Using a proactive approach, we involve teachers with the personal experience of a learning environment that is safe, stimulating, open, and challenging. Although education courses and seminars address innovative ways of teaching, most teachers teach the way they were taught without realizing the disconnect between what they claim to be their philosophy of education and their actual practice in the classroom. Our mindset, which is a composite of beliefs and values, filters and colors everything we do.

MINDSETS

Carol Dweck (2006) described two mindsets and their impact on learning. The "growth mindset" is grounded in a belief that growth is ongoing and that more effort will bring improved intelligence and performance. In contrast, a "fixed mindset" is grounded in a belief that "we are what we are," and it isn't likely to change. Those with a fixed mindset are apt to say things that define themselves unequivocally, like "I'm dumb" or "I'm not good at math," and use that as a reason to avoid learning. They are not likely to put effort into changing their viewpoint since they see it as unchangeable. Those who think they are smart may think they will always get good grades based on their native intelligence and unrelated to their effort.

Classrooms with positive learning environments use strategies that promote a growth mindset. Students' efforts are noticed and encouraged. Grades are not the focus as much as multiple indicators of ongoing learning. Mistakes are embraced as a step in the learning process. Misconceptions provide opportunities for dialogue and clarification. Questions from students give teachers feedback on their effectiveness in promoting growth.

As with the students, schools that promote developing growth mindsets and sharing among professionals create classrooms that promote learning.

Fixed mindsets occur across the learning spectrum from the very strong to the very weak students. With fixed mindsets, students are unwilling to take risks. They resist trying because they expect to fail no matter what they do. With growth mindsets, students are open to challenges and are willing to try new things because they are not afraid of making mistakes and focus on effort, expecting to improve if they work hard.

With students, the power to shape their perspective does rest with the teachers and their parents or other significant adults. By noticing the effort with statements like "wow, you really worked hard on that," the students who are working on establishing their identities will begin to focus on the effort and a belief that they can change. When adults say things like "wow, you are really smart" or "you're going to be the next LeBron James," they are focusing on the outcomes and may stifle growth.

Mindsets become a focus for teachers, too. Teachers with a fixed mindset are less likely to engage with their peers in professional learning communities where they examine their teaching and assessment strategies. As with the students, schools that promote developing growth mindsets and sharing among professionals create classrooms that promote learning.

Developing a learning classroom means focusing on creating a growth mindset as well as keeping the brain in the game. Good teachers implement strategies that engage students' brains while developing good relationships. That's where focus on developing relationships, relevance, and rigor changes things. When students are afraid, they are not fully using the part of their brains that allows them to learn. Instead, they remain stuck in their *lizard brain*. In addition to avoiding the lizard brain, this also means making sure the students understand its significance.

UNDERSTANDING THE IMPORTANCE OF THE SURVIVAL REFLEX TO TEACHING

The lizard brain is the most primitive part of the brain shared with other living creatures (including reptiles like lizards) and is focused on survival. Comprised primarily of the cerebellum and the brain stem, it keeps various bodily systems working. When we feel threatened, it becomes the primary focus for our autonomic system to work efficiently and activate our fight-or-flight response. Although this is critical for our survival, reacting can be problematic when we engage these defensive reflexes inappropriately in situations incorrectly perceived as threats due to our past experiences.

For example, Perry walks into his math class. He heads straight to the back of the classroom where the teacher is less likely to see him. He expects to be embarrassed in this class because he has often heard that he is a poor math student. Although his survival isn't really threatened, his experience says that he is likely to be humiliated, which for Perry is a very real and meaningful threat. He hides as much as he can in the class.

In a similar way, the teacher spots Perry, sees what appears to be an angry young man, and decides he better get him under control. His perception of Perry is based on his experience with other students who looked and acted similarly. He engages his defenses in order to survive also and not be humiliated by a difficult student. He puts his sights on Perry and decides to gain control of him from the beginning. He's in "fight" mode. Very little teaching and learning can take place when both the teacher and the learner are engaged in survival thinking and not accessing their reflective brains to make meaning and solve problems. We need to feel safe in order to fully access these areas.

This reality is exacerbated in schools where the students' brains are still developing through adolescence. Positron-emission tomography (PET) scans reveal that adolescent brains are most active in the feeling area when confronted with a problem. In contrast, adult brains are most active in the frontal lobe where reasoning processes information.

> *Staying free of the lizard brain helps teachers focus on what is right for learning, not what they need to do to survive.*

What does this mean for teachers? It means that teaching and learning happens best in a nonthreatening environment. It also indicates how difficult it may be to understand what might feel threatening to each student. How can teachers possibly know? This is a key element in building relationships and developing a classroom for learning. The point is not to know everything initially about every student, but to establish a safe environment, design a learning profile for each student, and be attentive to early signs of disengagement.

In this book, we address using the whole brain for effective teaching and learning. Staying free of the lizard brain helps teachers focus on what is right for learning, not what they need to do to survive.

One of the critical elements of creating a learning classroom is making the process of learning transparent. Teaching the students about learning will help make them good collaborators in their own learning. This begins when we focus on learning and invite the students to explore how they learn as they discover new knowledge. When we use this information to plan and deliver high quality lessons, we have a well-developed learning classroom.

CREATING THE LEARNING ENVIRONMENT

Relevance in the classroom begins by creating a classroom environment where learning is clearly the goal. When the classroom doesn't openly embrace and facilitate learning, students are left to wonder what is expected. Here are a couple examples.

Jennifer walked into her fourth-grade class with all the excitement and misgivings that students have when they begin a school year. As she stepped inside, she noticed the pleasant upbeat music that was playing. She looked around and noticed the posters on the wall, the area reserved for student work, and an area for pictures and information about students in this class titled "All About Me." The back corner of the room had some carpet, bookracks, and some beanbag chairs. Jennifer began to relax as she noticed how easy it was going to be to find things. Space-saver boxes were on each set of four desks containing pencils, pens, sticky notes, index cards, and highlighters. Mrs. Allen smiled, walked over, and introduced herself. Jennifer felt welcome. The atmosphere was calm and pleasant, making Jennifer feel safe and excited. Her anxieties diminished.

Next door, Rebecca walked into her classroom. Desks were arranged theater style. The walls were bare. The teacher sat behind a cluttered desk working on her computer without acknowledging Rebecca when she entered. Rebecca felt nervous and guarded, not knowing what to expect.

These two scenarios illustrate very different approaches to setting up a learning environment. One creates a clear vision of what will happen in the classroom, the other leads to uncertainty. For learning to happen, there needs to be a feeling of safety. Having a clear vision of what might be expected, where materials are located, and a clear feeling that the teacher feels good about teaching and is excited about the students in this class goes a long way toward allaying fears. Students who feel safe and welcome are much more likely to be open to learning and being engaged in the classroom.

Teachers who develop effective learning environments establish a *learning momentum* from the moment the students enter the class. The idea of establishing a learning momentum means that everything about the classroom clearly communicates a focus on learning.

What might threaten our students' success? Consider the questions that come to mind whenever we enter a new situation. What is expected here? What will I need? Will it be provided? Will I have a chance for success? How will I be treated? Am I going to be bored or excited when I come here? Does the teacher like me? Is the teacher fair? In addition to these issues, there are always those things that may happen outside of the classroom that threaten our students' safety. How will I be able to focus with these other things on my mind?

Teachers who focus on developing a classroom for learning take time before school starts to learn about students who will be in their class and reflect on how to build relationships and how to carefully plan instruction that is rigorous and relevant. The goal is also to encourage thinking and learning on an ongoing basis.

THE PROCESS OF DEVELOPING A LEARNING CLASSROOM

This is just the beginning of creating a classroom for learning. The process includes many aspects that go beyond what is typically considered when the focus is on managing a classroom. For instance, in addition to the elements just described, it also means paying attention to how teachers ask questions and how they respond to students. It means doing everything possible to engage students' brains during instruction. It also means establishing procedures and responses to behavior that promote learning and avoid punishment or rigidity that stifles growth. Differentiation and assessment become critical aspects of establishing a learning classroom because they make success available to all students.

In a learning classroom, our role as a teacher changes from delivering information to facilitating learning. To do this, we have to be *professional learners* who are constantly researching and reflecting to improve our practice. It is much better to proactively plan for developing an environment for learning than it is to just manage with a focus on reactive responses to misbehavior. Keeping learning at the forefront is the crucial element that differentiates the two. Chart 1.1 illustrates some of the differences between developing a learning classroom and managing a classroom.

Chart 1.1   Developing a Learning Classroom vs. Managing a Classroom

Developing a Learning Classroom	*Managing a Classroom*
Proactive thinking with emphasis on learning	Reactive thinking with emphasis on control
Relaxed, open, self-controlled	Rigid, oppressive, controlled
Safe to take risks	Fearful of taking risks
All thinking valued	Correct answers valued
Student centered, every student included in discussion, each has a role, a voice	Teacher centered, lectures, individual students called on
Open-ended questions	Closed, one right answer question to cover content
Paraphrased responses to clarify for understanding	Evaluated responses for correctness
Creative novel presentations to engage mind and emotions for learning	Sterile, boring presentation of facts to be remembered
Creating meaning, discovery, cognitive engagement	Telling meaning, emphasis on covering content

REFLECTION

After reading this chapter, take a few minutes to reflect on the following:

- Reflect on a classroom in which you felt you learned the most. What do you notice about that classroom as you think about it? What are the characteristics of that teacher's approach that facilitated your learning?
- Now consider someone in your life, teacher or other person, from whom you learned some important lessons. What made that relationship one which nurtured learning?
- Think about your classroom or your prospective classroom. In what ways have you established an environment that is safe for learning? Which of your current practices may inhibit learning?
- Reflect on your classroom setting. What might a student notice when entering your classroom? How will this perception enhance safety and promote learning?
- Think about a classroom in which you felt a sense of comfort when you entered it. What about that classroom made you feel that way?

ACTION

- Take specific characteristics and practices that you noticed in the reflections and list them as the foundation for developing your classroom. Begin to examine ways in which you may incorporate these and journal your thoughts for future reference.
- Take a moment and notice those things that inhibit learning for you. List these to help you understand some practices to avoid or at least understand the impact they may have on learning.
- Draw a sketch (cartoon) of what a learning community classroom would look like. Share this with colleagues.
- Close the book and write a brief journal entry to document key points you take away from reading this chapter.
- Visit two classrooms and document three observations for each of the three Rs—relationships, relevance, and rigor.
- Write and date a short letter addressed to yourself: describe what you think a visitor would observe in your classroom in terms of relationships, relevance, and rigor. Seal it and file it in a place where you will open it six months from now.
- Identify colleagues whose classroom is well organized and stimulates student engagement. Visit it and notice what students' needs they took into account when organizing their classroom. Ask questions to discern how they made the decisions they made.

- In conversations with friends and colleagues, practice effective listening skills by slowing down, pausing before responding, and then paraphrasing their perspective before giving yours. Notice how it works.
- When responding to students, work on paraphrasing their answers both when working individually as well as whole class. Notice how this impacts participation and relationships with students.
- Identify some positive posters or signs to use in your classroom. Think also of signs that promote thinking such as "What do you see?"; "What do you notice?"; "What do you think?"; "What do you wonder?"; and so forth.

2

Who Am I Who Teaches?

How Knowing Oneself Impacts Practice

"We teach who we are."

—Betty K. Garner

Have you ever wondered why students behave differently with different teachers? Although we tend to attribute this to personality and compatibility issues, it goes much deeper than that. Who we are impacts how we teach. Students relate to us based on their perceptions of who we are. When we work with new teachers, we challenge them to become aware of their own *presence* with a classroom full of students. When we work with experienced teachers, we encourage them to reflect on what they do intentionally or intuitively to create those energizing learning moments when they are totally present and effective. This is often difficult because teachers tend to downplay the significance of *who* they are and how this affects their teaching. Presence is an intangible synthesis of who we are as a person, which permeates what we do and how we do it, including how we build relationships, make information relevant, and set rigorous expectations of excellence.

Teaching involves more than content knowledge and skill. It involves our whole being. Students have an uncanny ability to see through teachers. On the first day of class, they instinctively size up their teachers and make a series of snap judgments such as cares or doesn't care, nice or mean, likes me or doesn't, interesting or too hard, fun or boring, "with it" or "out of it." Jeff, a ten-year-old boy, explained how he carefully studied his teachers and looked behind their eyes to see what they were really like. Most students look for evidence of authenticity or integrity to determine if the teachers' actions are trustworthy and consistent with what they say.

To help teachers better understand *who* they are, we encourage them to reflectively explore indicators like their self-talk, hot buttons, life stressors, thoughts, feelings, biases, values, beliefs, balance, and strengths. These factors directly influence actions and interactions within the classroom. This is especially important for idealistic new teachers who come with a wealth of knowledge about learning theories, pedagogical strategies, curriculum content, philosophies of education, prepared lesson plans, enthusiasm, and confident dreams of success but who quickly encounter the disconnect between coursework and the realities of everyday teaching. It is also important for experienced teachers to seriously reflect on *who* they are when stress and disillusionment drain their energy and dissipate their dedication. In this chapter, we examine how to help teachers look within themselves and become effective teachers and learners with their students throughout their lifetime.

SELF-TALK

Taking time to examine our inner dialogue helps us become aware of what drives our practice. Too often, this examination reveals that we focus on our weaknesses and fears more than our strengths.

In October, three new teachers gathered for their mentoring session with Roger, their administrator and coach. They expected to engage in a checklist report on what was going well and what needed improvement. Marilyn, a kindergarten teacher, was in her mid-forties. Because of layoffs, she made a career change. Carol, a third-grade teacher, and Mike, a fifth-grade teacher, were both fresh out of college and eager to make a good impression on their principal.

When they came together, Roger said, "Close your eyes and reflect on three to five things you most often say to yourself." The teachers looked cautiously at each other. Roger added, "You're not being graded and it is up to you if you want to share. I just ask you to be honest with yourself. Reflect a few minutes, then write down what you say to yourself." They began to write. Roger did the same.

To break the ice, he started, "I wrote, 'What can I do to help,' 'I can't be everywhere at once,' and 'What if they find out I am not sure what to do.'" The teachers were a little surprised at the last comment.

Mike said, "But you always act like you're so sure of yourself."

Roger smiled, "I know there's room for improvement. I also know I am sometimes afraid of making mistakes in judgment. I feel like this limits my freedom to act." The teachers were disarmed by Roger's honesty and openness in front of them.

Marilyn said, "I am constantly telling myself I'm not good enough; everyone else seems to catch on so much quicker."

"What does that tell you about yourself?" asked Roger.

"I guess I want everything to be perfect, so I won't be criticized or embarrassed." She paused. "You know what—I have never said that out loud or realized how often I thought about it before."

Roger asked, "What would be different if you accepted yourself as a learner?"

"I would be more relaxed and willing to take risks," Marilyn replied.

The teachers were becoming more relaxed and willing to share, knowing that they would benefit from a newfound awareness of what influences their actions and decisions.

Mike spoke up, "I wrote, 'I hope the kids don't ask me something I don't know the answer to.'"

By now the teachers were smiling as they realized everyone had underlying issues that could only be resolved if they brought them to a level of consciousness and admitted the power these issues had over them personally.

Carol said, "I wrote, 'I've got too much to do and not enough time.'"

"I wrote that too," said Mike.

"Me too," said Marilyn.

"What does that tell you?" asked Roger.

"That we all have too much to do and not enough time!" said Mike. They laughed, relieved that they could freely express themselves.

"And . . ." said Roger.

"And I have to be better organized," said Marilyn, "maybe think about what is really important rather than trying to rush through everything."

"Wow," said Carol, "you mean I could decide how to use my time?"

Roger said, "You are the professional. As a teacher and as a learner, you have to use the required curriculum as a guide and decide how to best share what is important. I encourage you to be aware of what you're thinking and saying to yourself and why you make the decisions you make. Keeping a reflective journal helps you be honest with yourself and continue to grow." He added, "Developing a meaningful relationship with students depends on how we think about them, because our thoughts determine how we feel about them, talk with or about them, and interact with them."

Roger met regularly with groups of new teachers and with experienced teachers to help them reflect on their self-talk and how it influences what they do. He encouraged all teachers to notice the difference when they focused on saying positive things about their own and their students' strengths instead of focusing on negative things like fears and shortcomings.

Discussions of this type are integral in developing professional learning communities and classrooms where learning is the focus. When teachers reach this level of self-awareness, they begin to honestly explore other aspects of who they are, like hot buttons.

HOT BUTTONS

Hot buttons are specific vulnerabilities rooted in past similar situations. They affect our thoughts, decisions, actions, interactions, words, and emotions. Cooper and McCoy (1999) clarify "hot buttons" like this: "Consider the button that operates an elevator and the one that detonates a nuclear bomb. Both look pretty much the same, but pressing each one causes a dramatically different reaction!" (p. 80). It's not the button, but what it is wired to. This perspective helps teachers understand why some insignificant incident can cause a disproportionate emotional response.

> A critical premise is that anger directed at another person is almost always connected to either hurt or fear.

Typically, hot buttons are wired to experiences from the teachers' families of origin or some other significant emotional experience. For example, Dan grew up with a father who was very loving but had a difficult time with anger. Consequently, whenever Dan got angry as a child, his dad would do whatever he could to make Dan laugh. This made Dan feel ridiculed and embarrassed, even though that was not his father's intent. So, later as a father himself, when Dan's daughter smiled or rolled her eyes when he was angry, he found himself becoming enraged way out of proportion to the event. He was actually feeling just like he did as a child, regressing to that time when he felt ridiculed. When he walked away after an outburst, he wondered what happened there.

Finding hot buttons requires an astute ability to listen within and notice the ebbs and flows of emotions felt in a given day. What triggers anger? Hurt? Fear? These are important questions for teachers to examine and answer in order to keep their brains working at maximum efficiency. A critical premise is that *anger directed at another person is almost always connected to either hurt or fear.* So, when teachers find themselves feeling anger that seems out of proportion to the situation, it is time to ask, "What hurt is this causing?" or "What is scaring me?"

Hot buttons are a shortcut to the lizard brain. As discussed previously, when this part of the brain is engaged, we are apt to act as if our survival is threatened, even when what is happening is only an approximation of what may have happened in the past. The lizard brain blocks the use of the reflective brain (Willis, 2006). The reflective brain is unique to humans; it promotes reasoning and creates meaning for learning.

Events perceived as threats to our survival engage the cerebellum and brain stem to make sure we keep alive through the fight, flight, or freeze response. It is critical to respond to threats; however, when there is no immediate threat but only the appearance of one, the excessive reaction is inappropriate.

Unless teachers are aware of their hot buttons, they become victims of their own emotional reactions. Incidentally, students of all ages, especially those who want to stir things up and avoid work, are very good at quickly detecting those things that trigger a reaction from the teacher. It is helpful to discuss these issues with a mentor or a group of trusted friends before incidents occur. Defusing hot buttons requires some specific steps:

1. *Recognition*—noticing that something is creating a reaction that is out of proportion to the event

2. *Introspection*—examining the past to see when something similar may have occurred, that is, when a similar feeling was triggered

3. *Reframing*—reflecting on how this past experience is coloring current situations and recognizing what is different

4. *Programming different responses*—slowing down responses when these feelings are triggered, so the brain has an opportunity to reason what is actually happening and that it is different than the historical experience

These steps take time to follow. This is why learning to pause and reflect when anger seems to be building is critical. It is during this pause that we can notice what is happening and begin reframing the experience. Since hot buttons often stem from past experiences, we need to examine our personal family history.

FAMILY OF ORIGIN

As creatures of habit, we develop patterns of behavior to deal with various situations. Sometimes, these habitual behaviors interfere with our ability to relate to students and colleagues.

Although most families are dysfunctional at some level, those who grow up in *chronically stressed families* (Cooper & McCoy, 1999) may be unaware that their coping behaviors are a source of stress for themselves and those around them. To survive chronic stressors like alcoholism or drug abuse, prolonged illness, death of a family member, loss of a job, homelessness, constant fighting, physical, emotional, or sexual abuse, and so forth.

children adapt as best they can. For example, they may take on the role of a surrogate parent to care for other siblings, withdraw to become invisible and prevent abuse, become aggressive or defiant to counter feelings of hurt, or try to keep the peace at all costs. Once entrenched, these survival strategies become normal for them, and they continue to use these strategies even when the stressor is no longer present.

For teachers, this may mean feeling a need to be perfect or to control others. It may also mean stuffing feelings or hiding in a crowd. Children who grow up in chronically stressed families often find themselves needing to learn to differentiate their adult lives from that which they experienced as children. Through reflective analysis and professional counseling, teachers are better able to recognize how these patterns are affecting their adult life and actively transform their way of thinking to allow them to be present in the moment. A way of framing this may be to remember this quote: "Scars remind us where we've been. They don't have to dictate where we are going."

Here are some examples of how these patterns show up in teacher situations. When Shawna was reprimanded for not calling a parent, she felt ashamed and devastated. It didn't matter that her principal was just pointing out a matter of procedure; the fact that she made a mistake was overwhelming to her. She found herself avoiding her principal and feeling like a child in his presence.

Rico found Ed to be a very abrasive person. Ed used sarcasm frequently. He was especially adept at put-down humor but always quick to say he was just joking. Rico didn't see it that way and was frequently hurt by Ed's comments. However, he pretended not to be bothered and kept his hurt inside.

It was difficult to have a discussion or disagreement with Anthony. Whenever confronted, no matter how softly, he became defensive and attacking. He fought hard to cover the insecurities he felt and the long-standing hurt he was feeling.

Given the opportunity to head her department, Julia ran with it. She found after a while that she was doing everything with little help from others. This evolved because she continually inserted herself into the work she delegated, causing others to feel discounted.

Rick seemed to enjoy life. No matter what went on, he smiled and laughed. On many occasions though, his laughter seemed inappropriate. He would make jokes about serious situations rather than engage in meaningful discussions. Others grew frustrated with his seeming inability to be serious. Privately, Rick often struggled with depression.

Each of these reactions is indicative of a pattern learned in chronically stressed families. For those entrenched in these patterns, their dysfunctional nature only becomes evident when their adult relationships misfire repeatedly for similar reasons. It often takes some outside help to examine the origin of the patterns and the rules that they adopted from their life experiences that governed these reactions. Some of these rules become evident in self-talk, illustrated as follows:

"My needs don't count."

"If I don't do it, it won't get done. Everything is my responsibility."

"I don't measure up."

"When I am funny, things feel better. Avoid sadness at all costs."

"Avoid conflict at all costs."

Earnie Larsen, a noted author in the field of codependence and founder of the Stage II Recovery program (see www.earnie.com for more information) that addresses these dynamics, said in his workshops that "fear looks back." When this happens, fear becomes debilitating. Vivid thoughts of similar past events caution us to be careful because these might create a similar outcome. However, each situation is different, and we need to slow down and examine the situation *as it is.* Then, taking the current circumstances into consideration as well as what was learned previously, we can move forward.

Establishing a support system is a way to help mitigate the role of growing up stressed. Everyone has a *family of chance.* This is the family into which we are born; however, everyone can also have a *family of choice.* This is a group of people who provide support and encouragement to nurture growth. Within this social context, we develop our personal biases, values, and beliefs that influence who we are and affect how we teach.

BIASES, VALUES, AND BELIEFS

Biases filter how information is perceived and processed. They are based on beliefs and values about how things should be and what we consider to be right/wrong or good/bad. For example, if we believe a quiet classroom is a sign of a good teacher and a noisy class indicates a bad teacher, we do all we can to maintain a quiet, controlled classroom and diligently work to avoid or minimize any commotion, talking, or peer interactions. If we value correct responses to our questions more than students' questioning the relevance of what we present in class, we tend to give better grades to students who do exactly what they are told and subtly discourage creative thinkers who suggest different ways of doing things.

Our biases become problematic when we are not aware of them. For example, Charlese did not realize how she was instinctively repulsed when one of her students came to school with dirty clothes. Her subtle body language sent the message that she wanted to avoid being around him. Only when she became aware of her own biases was Charlese able to change her reactions, investigate her student's situation, and get him the help he needed.

Biases that originate from our childhood or from traumatic experiences can be deeply embedded. For example, if we were raised in families that held prejudiced views of people from different races, lifestyles, religions, ethnic, or socioeconomic backgrounds, we need to examine how these influence our relationships with students and our effectiveness as a teacher. Even if we choose as adults to hold different views, biases can subtly creep into our thoughts and actions. They can be very pervasive and distort intended meanings of communications with administrators, parents, colleagues, and students. They tend to become evident when we make snap judgments without reflective consideration. Biases can also be positive filters that make us feel drawn toward specific characteristics in others. As we become aware of our biases, we are able to redirect or change them for our benefit.

We all hold values and beliefs that affect our perspective on life. They filter how we perceive and process information and are so embedded in our thinking that we are often unaware of their presence. Students frequently mirror the values and beliefs of their parents and peers. It is pleasant to work in situations where educators, parents, and community share common beliefs and values. However, with the diversity of most communities, this is rarely the case. Students may come to school with values and beliefs that are contrary to what we are trying to instill through our teaching. For example, if parents tell their children that they were no good at math or reading, they are conveying that it is acceptable or normal not to like these subjects. Joe, a sixth grader, was sent to the office for fighting. When questioned about his inappropriate behavior, Joe responded, "My dad said if somebody hits me I should pick up a board and hit 'em harder! That's what I did!" Teenage peers can encourage behaviors based on beliefs and values that undermine what we value: for example, they may think it is cool to get away with cheating, to be tough by bullying others, or to prove their independence by defiantly arguing with the teacher.

When doing professional development seminars, we ask participants to write their definitions of teaching and learning. An analysis of what they write quickly reveals underlying beliefs about teaching and learning. If teachers believe their job is transmitting information, they work very hard to present clear explanations to help students remember what is taught. If teachers believe learning is created by the learner, their instructions facilitate students' ability to gather and process information, to question, research, and problem solve, so they can make sense for themselves and apply the information for life. Too often, we hear teachers say they are teaching something because it is in the curriculum, it will be on the test, or it is necessary for the next grade level.

While teaching, we are making thousands of decisions every day. It is challenging to unpack the underlying biases, values, and beliefs that influence those decisions. When teachers feel they are in a rut or getting burned out, we encourage them to do reflective journaling and honestly evaluate why they do what they do. We can only change what we are aware of. It is also helpful to share with trusted colleagues who are willing to go deeper and facilitate discussion of biases, values, and beliefs that affect our actions, thoughts, and feelings.

THOUGHTS AND FEELINGS

Although thoughts seem to have a life of their own, we have the power to control and guide our thoughts. How we think about ourselves and how we envision our role as a teacher directly impacts how we act in the classroom; how we prepare and present lessons; and how we build relationships with students, colleagues, administrators, and parents. Thoughts are powerful assets that can energize or become hidden land mines that sabotage efforts to develop a learning classroom. Thoughts and feelings are so intimately connected that it is often difficult to tell which is which.

> *Positive visualizations release endorphins in the brain and stimulate related positive feelings.*

Thoughts frequently take the form of visualization. We use visualization in a broad sense of mental representation of images, sounds, feelings, smells, touch, symbols, and so on. Positive visualizations release endorphins in the brain and stimulate related positive feelings. Negative mental images, in the form of stress and worry, also release chemicals in the brain causing anxiety and depression. Many people think they have little or no control over their thoughts and feelings. Susan began to realize she actually had the power to regulate her thoughts in a way that would affect how things went during the day. She wrote in her journal:

This morning, I tried it for the first time and it really worked! The last two weeks were really tough. I found myself lying awake at night worrying about everything—was I really cut out for this job? What am I doing wrong? I never get done. The kids are rowdy and disrespectful. I'm exhausted! Today, when I got up, I decided I was going to follow my mentor's suggestion and I consciously decided to have a good day. I closed my eyes and pictured my students working with me, participating in class, and enjoying our time together. Around noon, I realized the morning had gone well. I smiled as I pictured the afternoon classes also going well. And they did! Wow! I plan to keep doing this every day!

Without realizing it, we can spend most of our time thinking about problems and all that can go wrong rather than thinking about what we are grateful for and how things could go well. Coaches in track and field remind hurdlers to focus on the finish line rather than the hurdles. Focusing on the hurdles results in hitting them. The same is true for teachers. Olympic athletes undergo extensive training in visualization to picture perfect accomplishment of their activity. Lamar asked his inner-city tenth graders to picture themselves in ten years. About half the students saw themselves doing some sort of job. Only three saw themselves going to college. The others said they could not see that far ahead. Needless to say, Lamar found this disturbing and initiated a daily exercise of visualizing possibilities for the future. We need to focus on our goals and visualize how we want it to be in order to be able to make that happen.

What we say and do is based on what we think and feel. Jim, a second grader, had a terrible reputation for disrupting class with his outbursts of anger and was frequently assigned to in-school suspension because of this and other inappropriate behaviors. After working with an intervention specialist, he suddenly had a compelling insight. He said, "I think I've got this figured out. If I change my thoughts, my actions change themselves. You know it's easier to change my thoughts." From that day on, he was seldom in any kind of trouble. Such a powerful insight is rare even for adults. We become what we think about.

On occasion, teachers get so frustrated that they regularly vent a torrent of negative feelings, especially in the teachers' lounge (workroom). When this happens on a regular basis, the school climate is polluted with a haze of pessimistic criticism that generates destructive negative energy. We encourage teachers to protect themselves when they are around "negaholics" by being aware of their own thinking and choosing to neutralize the negativity with positive thoughts and comments. If we don't let negative things get inside our mind, we don't have to vent to let them out. No one can steal our joy unless we let them.

BALANCE

In order to really know who we are as a teacher, we have to maintain a balance between our personal and professional lives. We also have to be healthy in body, soul, and spirit. This involves an ongoing process of self-reflection that empowers teachers to use their creativity to enhance who they are as a person, a teacher, and a learner.

We encourage teachers to take care of their body by getting a good night's sleep, eating healthy, exercising, and making sure they drink lots of water. Taking care of their mind involves intentional exploration of new ideas, ongoing professional development, in-depth dialogue with colleagues about educational research, and keeping up with technology to facilitate learning.

Attending to the spirit is an essential aspect of life. The word *spirit* comes from the Latin *spiritus,* meaning breath or life. Because we encounter such diverse beliefs about spiritual matters and generally consider this to be a very private area, we tend to avoid the topic. However, we need to be in touch with our inner spirit to know who we are. We encourage teachers to achieve peace within, regardless of external factors, to maintain focus on what really matters in the midst of all the distracting noise and busyness that demand attention. Just like physical and mental health, spiritual health is essential for effective teaching and learning.

When we align body, soul, and spirit, we are balanced. This means we synchronize what we think with what we believe, with what we feel, with what we say, with what we do, and with who we are. When these are out of alignment, there is stress. Students know when we are for real. They know that we mean what we say and they can trust who we are.

Balance includes a meaningful and honest support system, which nurtures willingness to change, create, and learn in every aspect of life. This support system can also help teachers recognize harmful patterns, overcome obstacles, build on strengths, and develop a deeper understanding of our thinking and feelings as we work through issues. An overall plan to accomplish this healthy balance includes the following steps:

- Engage in reflective journaling designed to examine feelings and their origin, explore ideas and impulses, and identify strengths and biases.
- Identify those who will be positive supports and involve them as trusted resources. Be that trusted resource for them also. Having a mentor is an important part of this. Becoming a mentor models this for others.
- Examine physical and emotional health and make a plan to stay in control even when under stress. Make this plan explicit and keep track of your progress to help maintain motivation.
- Identify long-standing hurts and do what it takes to allow them to heal and to move on. In this process, it may also be necessary to forgive oneself. Remember to "treat yourself as you would your best friend."

Developing a learning classroom begins with humble willingness to honestly examine areas in which we struggle as well as areas in which we excel. To have meaningful relations with students and colleagues, we first have to have a meaningful relationship with ourselves.

STRENGTHS

Strengths are characteristics or attributes that enhance capabilities. To avoid appearing boastful, teachers sometimes downplay their strengths rather than accentuating them for further improvement. Without realizing it, we develop a mindset that focuses on identifying weaknesses and trying to fix them. This also applies to our interactions with students and to our assessment of their work. Instead of trying to avoid mistakes in teaching, take some time to assess ways to develop and use personal strengths. We tend to focus on tasks and trying to be good at doing something rather than recognizing how our inner strengths, guiding principles, and core values directly affect how we think, feel, and act in every situation. Some of these include character traits like honesty (with ourselves and others), willingness to learn, trustworthiness, ethics, generosity, tolerance, kindness, caring, wisdom, courage, patience, humor, creativity, flexibility, perseverance, commitment, and respect.

When we coach experienced teachers preparing for their National Board Certification and advanced specialist degrees, we see how difficult it is for them to identify and discuss their strengths or their basic core values and beliefs that drive their practice. Once they become aware of why they do what they do, they are able to change themselves, take charge of their own professional development, and focus on developing their strengths rather than depending on external evaluation to point out what needs to be improved. Our ability to accept students for who they are relates directly to our ability to accept ourselves.

CLOSING THOUGHTS

We teach who we are. From the moment we step across the threshold of our home and leave for school, we carry with us who we are. This includes all of our experiences, knowledge, skills, values, beliefs, feelings, and personal baggage. Self-awareness directly influences classroom development and student learning by giving us the freedom to choose how we interact with students and colleagues. Without self-awareness, we become victims of subtle influences that affect our choices and actions. Students look for authenticity and are more willing to build trusting relationships with teachers who are real. Relationships are the foundation of effective teaching and learning. See the summary of differences in Chart 2.1.

Chart 2.1   Contrasting Self-Awareness in a Learning vs. a Managed Classroom

Who You Are Within a Learning Classroom	*Who You Are Within a Managed Classroom*
Reflective self-awareness of who you are as a person and a professional	Focus on who you are as a professional
Sense of presence—authenticity; your whole being setting parameters in relation to content, context, and communication	Structure of system and position of authority setting parameters in relation to content, context, and communication
Willingness to be honest and admit mistakes	Fear of making mistakes or appearing weak
Aware of own hot buttons, biases, values, beliefs, feelings, and other personal issues that influence practice	Unaware of own hot buttons, biases, values, beliefs, feelings, and other personal issues that influence practice
Colearner with students	Dispenser of information
Focus on integrated balance in life; wellness in body, soul, and spirit	Focus on responding to demands of job and family, often out of balance
Reflective journal writing to identify patterns and questions and promote professional growth	Just keeping up with daily duties, no time to reflect and journal
Seeks wisdom, insights, and tips from experienced mentor or trusted colleagues	Prefers to do it alone to avoid appearing unable to handle situations

REFLECTION

- After reading this chapter, reflect on your approach to problems. What patterns do you notice emerging when you struggle with other people or with problems in your life? What strengths emerge?
- What are your first thoughts of the day as you prepare for class? How do these change throughout the day? How many are positive? How many are negative?
- When you think about what you say to yourself on an ongoing basis, what are the three things you most often say? What does this tell you?
- When you fail at something, how do you react? How might this impact your teaching?
- Examine your relationships with others. Are the people who surround you supportive of your growth? What evidence do you have of their willingness to be honest and sensitive with you when it comes to issues that might impact your growth?

- Describe how you feel and the thoughts you have when you enter a classroom to teach. Where are you looking when you begin to teach? What may affect your confidence when you are teaching?
- What are your underlying biases, values, and beliefs that drive your practice? Which of these are productive and encourage learning? Which are counterproductive?

ACTIONS

- Document what you do to take care of your physical health. Create a written plan to monitor your eating habits, exercise, and sleep. Make it a practice to monitor yourself on a regular basis in each of these areas and record your progress in meeting your goals.
- Write three to five things you say to yourself most often during any given day. What does this tell you about yourself?
- Write a description of what you would want others to remember about you as a person and as a professional. Compare how these characteristics align with who you are now.
- Make a list of your most frequently experienced emotions and when they occur. Examine emotional health and look for unresolved or ongoing issues that interfere with your ability to focus. Make a written plan for addressing these and letting them go.
- Examine your spiritual life. Spend some quiet time in meditation and reflection to experience inner peace. Notice what robs you of your peace. Make a list of times you felt deep joy. Make a written plan for maintaining focus and inner peace.
- Examine how you sustain your knowledge and understanding of your teaching. Create a process for your ongoing development. Keep track of your progress and journal what you learn.
- Build a support group who will honestly give you feedback, encouragement, challenges, and opportunities for personal and professional growth.

3

Who Are the Students We Teach?

How Knowing Our Students Affects Teaching and Learning

"They don't care what we know until they know that we care."

—*Madeline Hunter*

Janet entered the classroom quietly. She scanned the room and found a desk that was unoccupied with no one sitting near it yet. She sat down and looked at her desk. She really wanted to be invisible. As the other students entered, she busied herself with getting her books out, seeming to be focused on getting ready for class. In fact, she was building a safe place for herself by avoiding interactions with the other students. Most ignored her. Those who said "hi" got a polite smile and a nod. Janet's mind was not on learning; it was on survival. She felt that she didn't fit in. There were a lot of reasons for this, but no one ever seemed to care what was going on with her. As long as she did her work and didn't bother anyone, no one bothered her, including the teacher.

Cynthia virtually danced into the room. Her presence seemed to require a spotlight. She spoke loudly, laughed a lot, and seemed to be very happy. Others deferred to her and seemed to admire her. She didn't work very hard in school, but that didn't seem to matter because she was so popular.

Interestingly, both Cynthia and Janet may be dealing with similar situations in their lives that require them to find ways to adapt. One chose to hide; the other found that being the center of attention worked for her. In these situations, however, teachers face a challenge. How can they know what might be impacting a student's behavior? And when should they intervene? Who are these kids anyway?

UNDERSTANDING UNIQUENESS

We all know students are different, but what does that really mean? Kindergarten teachers are amazed at the uniqueness of each little child entering school. They can immediately tell which children come from unruly daycare centers, which come from homes where parents spent time conversing and playing with their children, which come with background knowledge about numbers and the alphabet, and which have little familiarity with anything related to school. Some children catch on quickly and some don't seem to have a clue what they are doing. As children get older, their differences exponentially amplify with the complexities of personal experiences. Middle and high school students clearly demonstrate the extent of these differences in knowledge, skills, abilities, attitudes, personalities, effort, motivation, aspirations, and opportunities.

One of the most common complaints we hear from teachers at all levels is, how can I possibly meet the needs of each individual student? Without realizing it, teachers often fall into a mindset of teaching the *class*—an assorted group of same-age students assigned together at a given time. Somehow the individuals get swallowed up in a current of overwhelming stress. Although teachers try to differentiate instruction, they easily succumb to the constraints of scheduling, pressures of curriculum coverage, and demands of standardized testing requirements. In Chapters 5 and 6, we address instructional planning, implementation, and assessment; here we want to focus on *who* we are teaching.

To teach effectively, we must make every effort to get to know each student. Sometimes, this involves looking past external characteristics and accepting individuals for who they are. It means suspending judgment and projecting positive expectations. There is a delicate balance between researching past history of students and keeping an open mind to let students reveal who they are. The old adage, "forewarned is forearmed," is both beneficial and detrimental. Prior knowledge about students from records and previous teachers can filter and skew perceptions and expectations of students before teachers even meet them. On the other hand, it is important to know vital medical information and specific needs or conditions affecting students. In both cases, we need to be reflectively aware of personal experiences that may bias how we may view students. We need to be cautious in weighing this information.

It is natural to be more attracted to some students than to others. However, all students (yes, even those we can't stand) are sacred, full of valuable potential and resources. Students are aware of how teachers think and feel about them. They are adept at reading adults—the way teachers look at them, say their name, accept them, correct them, and encourage them. The teachers' attitude and actions reflect their values and beliefs about who they are and who they think their students are. Students listen more with their hearts than with their heads. How they perceive *what they think the teacher feels about them* determines how they work with the teacher and accept what he or she offers.

Early in the school year, Danielle got herself in hot water with her teacher, Ms. Wilson. In spite of numerous requests from the teacher to be quiet, she kept whispering to her best friend. They had things that they believed really needed to be discussed right then! Nevertheless, the teacher was upset at what she viewed as disrespect. Not knowing Danielle well, this disrespectful behavior led the teacher to see Danielle as being a disrespectful person.

Knowing and understanding our students stimulate more engaging, relevant learning and more highly motivated learners.

When Danielle came into the room as the year progressed, she noticed the teacher's lack of patience with her. It seemed to Danielle that, whenever she messed up, it was always noticed and addressed in front of the class. She heard the exasperation in the teacher's voice. Initially, she tried to fix things, but being a social person, she often found herself talking when she wasn't supposed to. It seemed to Danielle that she couldn't do anything right. After a while, she began believing that Ms. Wilson just didn't like her and that there was nothing she could do. Danielle lost energy for the class, shutting down and doing what she could to just get through. Her feelings about school in general deteriorated. She also lost energy for trying to get Ms. Wilson to like her.

In this situation, Danielle's perceived disrespect translated into her being viewed as disrespectful. This perspective then meant that the teacher viewed all of Danielle's behavior through this lens. It made it difficult for Danielle to break out of the mold that she inadvertently created. Ultimately, it was Danielle's perception of Ms. Wilson's perspective of her that was the primary reason for her lagging performance in the class. It really didn't matter if Ms. Wilson actually liked Danielle or not; Danielle believed she didn't, so she didn't.

So, what can teachers do to better understand who they teach and begin the process of developing relationships with them? This question underlies the whole process of teaching and learning. Knowing and understanding our students stimulate more engaging, relevant learning and more highly motivated learners. When they know that teachers care, they care what they know!

GETTING TO KNOW OUR STUDENTS

A sixth grader explained the difference between knowing someone and *knowing* someone. The emphasis she put on the second knowing was her way of enlightening her teacher to the subtleties of what it means to *know* someone. She said, "Teachers don't have a clue who the kids are! All they want to know is how smart they are. It's like you really get to know someone when you do things together and talk to each other and find out if you can depend on them when things get tough." Great teachers do this. Those who don't are usually so busy trying to be fair in treating everyone alike that they overlook the unique treasures each student has to offer.

Many classes begin with an overview of the course, what is expected, what will impact the final grade, and how students must behave in the class. All of this may appear to be the foundation for learning, but it's not. It is just an overview of what will happen without asking or seeking to understand what will impact the journey of the students (learners). In the following sections are suggested ways to get to know our students.

Understand Learning Styles

Imagine a class where the first thing the teacher sought to know was how the students learned. In the process of developing a classroom, this is one of the first tasks teachers initiate to help them plan lessons. Students are encouraged to self-assess how they learn best and their role in the instructional process

Students who are encouraged to examine how they learn take a different view of the process in the classroom. Many classes begin with an overview of the course, what is expected, what will impact the final grade, and how students must behave in the class. All of this may appear to be the foundation for learning, except it's not. It is just an overview of what will happen without asking or seeking to understand what will impact the journey of the students (learners). Here are some tools to learn this information.

Student Survey

To teach the whole child, it is important to identify students' interests, strengths, needs, and capabilities as soon as possible. A carefully worded student survey is one way to get to know students (see samples in Appendixes A and B). Questions on the surveys can be used several ways; for example, they can be used separately for a daily "quick write" activity on index cards; they can be printed as an activity sheet and given to the whole class at once; or they can be used as discussion points with individuals or small groups. Keep in mind that older students may be cautious about giving too much information until they know and trust their teacher. This is why we recommend doing two surveys: introductory student survey (initial contact) and advanced student survey (after a few weeks of contact). With younger children (preK through second grade), we recommend weaving the questions into individual talking times within the context of daily interactions. Be sure to make notes—sticky notes with simple coding system work well.

Beginning of the Year "Talking Stick" Group

One powerful way for students to share how they learn best and to get to know each other is using the Native American talking stick. While sitting in a circle, students pass a decorated stick (or other symbol) from person to person to indicate whose turn it is to talk. The teacher explains that the person with the stick is the only one who may talk while others listen intently and respectfully. Listening skills need to be practiced. As the stick is passed, students share their thoughts about a specific topic or respond to a prompt question. The teacher may paraphrase to ensure understanding. This activity demonstrates the importance of each student and validates that their contributions to the group are valued. When the exercise is completed, a good summarizing question may be, what did you notice about the students in this class? This provides an opportunity to discuss diversity within the group and emphasizes the importance of learning with and from each other. The process may be replicated often to address needs, concerns, feelings, or issues within the class or in other situations. This kind of activity helps students develop empathy and affiliation, which are learned skills that "can be developed through experience and feedback in close-knit, interactive groups where students learn how to use feedback to develop trusting friendships" (Jensen, 2011, p. 129).

Student List of Needs From Teacher and Classmates

Another way to get to know students is to ask them to individually write a list of *what they need from you and what they need from their classmates to help them be successful.* We encourage students to be honest and explain that we will collect and compile a list of their items without sharing their names. Then we distribute the compiled list for students to classify, analyze, and discuss the items on the list. Responses vary with age levels, but some themes tend to appear, for example, do more hands-on activities, assign less work, give more free time, go slower, explain better, show you care, smile a little, let us work with our friends, make things interesting, talk about what is relevant to us, keep up with what is going on in our lives, and so forth. When students write something we don't agree with or don't like to hear, we need to reflect on why and how we react. If we want students to take risks and really say what they are thinking, we must respect their comments without taking things too personally.

Ongoing Assessment

We frequently use formal and informal ongoing assessment methods to identify and monitor students' level of understanding. This includes doing a brief pretest of skill and knowledge levels in content areas. This information is closely related to the learning objectives and becomes a valuable resource for identifying growth over time. We use standardized test results and other available data to analyze progress based on local, state, and national norms. Assessment is discussed in more detail in Chapter 6. We caution teachers that some curriculum requirements for data collection can be overly demanding on our time and energy. Some approaches, such as "running notes," Response to Intervention (RTI), Reading Recovery, and others, become easier once the "coding" systems are mastered.

It is easy to fall into the trap of identifying who students are in relation to their grades. One fifth grader said, "The teacher never tests me on what I really know." We need to consider multiple ways for students to demonstrate what they know. Learning has to do with life, not just schoolwork. It is sometimes challenging to stay focused on who we are teaching when students appear to be lazy or unmotivated, and we have to give them bad grades. We encourage teachers to remember that students who avoid work usually do not understand the work. They might say it is boring, or they just don't want to do it because they don't care, but these may be evasive maneuvers they learn very early to avoid being embarrassed or admitting they don't understand. It is also possible, however, that they are bored because they understood this at the beginning and didn't need to go over it again. In either case, more data are needed to understand the needs of the student.

Assessment includes more than paper-pencil or computer-generated tests. It also involves learning to become a professional "kid watcher." By recognizing misconceptions, learning gaps, and error patterns, we can provide appropriate assistance. Other factors to be assessed include variables like attendance, class participation, interest, levels of engagement, attitudes, motivation, self-correction, initiative, work completion, effort, self-directed research, cooperation, collaboration, transfer, application, questioning, and curiosity. These all play a vital part in revealing who the students are, their comprehension, and their responsiveness to the teacher's assistance.

We avoid putting too much emphasis on things like IQ scores that were never meant to be a static assessment of one's intelligence. They give data about a student at a point in time. They can inform teachers about existing deficiencies, but they do not reveal a student's potential to understand.

In the end, the teachers' expectations for students need to be higher than what the students expect of themselves. Learning has more to do with how students go about creating meaning for themselves than with IQ scores, grades, or standardized test scores.

Responsive Journal Writing

Various forms of responsive journal writing are powerful tools to get to know students. This practice can easily be incorporated into every content area at every grade level. At the end of a lesson, we invite younger students to draw something they learned or wondered about in relation to what they did in class. When introducing this practice, we take time to clarify a few things. For example, journaling does not mean writing a log of what they did; it is a reflection on what they learned and what they were thinking. We ask them to respond to questions such as the following: What sense did you make of this? What does this mean to you—in your own words? What questions come to mind in relation to this information? Too often, teachers feel so pressured to cover content that they teach right up to the end of time allotted for the class and give a quick assignment as students are ready to move to the next lesson. When we invite students to write a *brief* reflection, we give them an opportunity to stop and reflect on the essence of the lesson, process the information for meaning, integrate it into their knowledge base, and generate questions for further learning. Without this reflective time, students are continually inundated with a flood of information, most of which is washed away by the next stream of new information. It is very important to respond promptly to these writings. Usually, one or two words or a short sentence of encouragement or acceptance is enough to acknowledge or validate students' remarks. Because teachers in middle and high school have so many students a day, we suggest using index cards or half-sheets of paper for daily reflections and notebooks for weekly, more in-depth, reflective writing. We assure students that we will never share what they have written without their permission. Depending on their level of trust, students will go deeper in sharing their learning journey. At times, we have students write reflections without signing their name, or make it optional to sign their names. Some students might be more honest if they write anonymously. This quick activity assesses what is important to the students, helps us get to know them better, and gives immediate feedback on the lesson. It also empowers the students to participate in developing a learning community and helps us become more effective teachers.

> *What sense did you make of this? What does this mean to you—in your own words? What questions come to mind in relation to this information?*

One perspective that may help understand the importance of reflection to the learning process is to think of learning as a trip through the woods.

The first time through is when we make a path focusing on each step until we reach the destination for that particular journey. Reflection is retracing that path, noticing the markers along the way, and having a chance to remember why we went this particular way. The second trip makes the path clearer and easier to find the next time we visit. This describes what happens in our brains too as we make neural connections and process new knowledge for future access.

Student Drawings

At every age level, we suggest inviting students to draw what school is like for them. Then we ask the students to talk about their picture with us or a group of peers. This approach helps students who have difficulty expressing what is going on inside their heads. Older students can write a title, description, or interpretation. Tony, a third-grade boy who was constantly getting in trouble for misbehavior, drew a pair of eyes on the left side of a paper with lines coming from the eyeballs to a stick figure of a person near the right side of the paper. He explained, "I wish other people could see things the way I see them." This opened a conversation about how he saw things and how some of his issues were related to the differences between his perceptions and his teachers' expectations. Carlos, a seventh grader who was always angry and disruptive, drew a picture of himself in full army fatigue uniform standing near the bottom middle of the paper and facing two attacking army tanks. In his hand, he had a peashooter held to his mouth. He explained that this is how helpless and defenseless he felt with school and home (the two tanks) attacking him on all sides. This young man was having a very difficult time emotionally and academically. After sharing his desperation, teachers and parents were able to lighten up on their criticism and pressure. They took a more supportive approach to help him deal with his issues. Through their nonverbal graphic renditions, students reveal windows into their thoughts and feelings that teachers might otherwise never see or hear about.

Drawing self-portraits is another way for students to give insight into how they see themselves. If students ask if they should draw a whole person or just the head, we tell them they can do whatever they prefer, what is important to them. For example, if they draw stylish clothes or a fancy hairdo, these are important to them. If they do not draw something, like ears, listening is not important. A variation of this approach is to ask the students to draw just their heads and what it would look like if they could see what is going on inside or have them draw a full figure doing their favorite activity or surrounded by their favorite things.

"Beautiful Thoughts" Activity

To get to know students, some teachers use a practice called "beautiful thoughts" at the beginning or end of a class to encourage students to be reflective. This simple activity invites students to be still, reflect, and wonder for a few seconds. It stimulates their imagination through visualization, helps them focus on something positive, and releases endorphins in their brain, which affect how they feel. It also provides a window into their lives and thinking. Many students will tell about some exciting event or special moment such as winning a sports event, getting a new pet, taking a trip, and so on, that helps the teacher get to know them better. With younger students, we recommend they *pair and share* their thoughts, so everyone gets an opportunity to speak. Then invite a few to share their thoughts with the whole group. With older students who might be a little self-conscious about sharing something personal, we recommend having them write or quickly illustrate their beautiful thoughts. Then the teacher collects what they wrote or drew and selects a few samples to share anonymously. It is also important for the teachers to share their beautiful thoughts to model many different examples of ways to reflect and wonder, so students get to know the teacher. Some teachers use guided imagery related to the lesson. Others have given the activity different names, for example, calling it a positive or happy thought, "vita-mind," or "energizer." We have used variations of this with students of all ages from preschool through graduate school.

GET TO KNOW STUDENTS' FAMILY BACKGROUND

Steve Hoelscher, Michigan former state director of the Schools to Watch program, repeatedly stated, "In schools, we control all the variables to make a student successful." Teachers who initially hear this typically object, vigorously stating, "We cannot control what happens at home." They are right. And they are wrong.

Steve isn't saying that teachers can control what happens at home. He is saying teachers control the variables that make students successful. One needs only to reflect on these questions to understand the wisdom of his comment:

- Do you know of a student who came from a troubled home and who succeeded?
- Do you know a student with a learning disability who succeeded?
- Do you know a student with a physical disability who succeeded?
- Do you know a student coming from an economically disadvantaged home who succeeded?

Confronted with these questions, teachers usually nod their heads to acknowledge they do know such students. When asked what made the difference, they typically answer, "A caring teacher." In many cases, they know this because they are speaking of themselves.

So what specifics do we need to know when it comes to students' family background? While it is helpful to know the family makeup, teachers must be cautious about judging a situation too quickly. Knowing a student's parents and guardians has a practical value in knowing who can support his or her learning. However, noticing the impact of the family on a student's emotional and physical health is also critical.

This begins with the recognition that students do not arrive at school with nothing on their minds. Do students come with high expectations or no expectations? Did they leave their homes with a kiss and a hug or a shout and a slap? Teachers need to know about family issues and situations that impact student learning; for example, do the students have one or two parents involved in their lives, are they in foster care or trapped in the turmoil of divorce and custody issues, or are they homeless or in need of social services? Whatever the situation, it will help teachers immensely to find ways to understand what is impacting their students and also to incorporate strategies that will bring them "into the room" and "leave their baggage" at the door as much as possible. Responsive journal writing can provide family information that impacts learning. Getting to know the parents and guardians builds a partnership to support students.

Build Relationship With Parents

Students live within complex family and social systems. What we experience with students in a school setting is only one facet of who they are. To get to know *who* we are teaching, we need to know something about our students' culture, family, friends, and community. This includes being familiar with local businesses, places of worship, community affairs, and issues that involve students and their families. When possible, we encourage participating in community events, afterschool activities, sports events, art or music presentations, and other areas where students are involved. It is often very revealing and helpful to get to know students on a personal level in these kinds of informal settings.

Students who speak a native language other than English at home have a different worldview. Sometimes young children with limited English serve as translators for their parents. Families also have to deal with complex social realities like translating official notices or documents, navigating immigration issues, and getting available services; becoming familiar with the schooling system; and fitting in with peer groups. To better understand the culture of these students, we need to find a way to learn about their language, customs, values, beliefs, and traditions. Participating in cultural gatherings can help gain an understanding of these students in a very personal way. When possible, we can provide translators for parent conferences and for important notices being sent home.

Most schools have open house or meet the teacher events near the beginning of the school year, as well as some kind of parent-teacher meetings throughout the year. Tom Hoerr (2012), a principal, author, and consultant describes how he gave an index card to parents and guardians at the first open house of the year. The card asked for responses to two questions: "What do you want for your child from our school? What's the one thing you want us to teach your child?" (p. 90). Hoerr stated that 20 percent of the returned cards said self-confidence was the one thing parents wanted for their child.

Some schools organize more frequent, informal coffees or focus groups to involve parents in discussions and policy decisions affecting them and their children. The important thing is building trust and cooperation between parents and teachers. If parents had an unpleasant schooling experience, they need encouragement to feel welcome at school. Often, angry parents are scared or hurt parents. Usually, the source of their fear or hurt is their own personal school experience.

Although making home visits can be challenging, it is a good way to get to know a student within the family setting. Entering their world helps us to see things from students' perspective. Because of limited budgets, teachers who make home visits often do them on their own time. We recommend pairing with a colleague when making visits. It is important to call the parents to make sure it is fine with them to visit and to set a time that is convenient for them. Sometimes parents have working schedules or family situations that make visits impractical.

A personal phone call to each family before the start of school is a great way to start out on a positive note. This is a way for teachers to let the family know who they are and to ask them what they think is important to know about their child—strengths, concerns, interests, medical issues, hopes, and dreams. Investing this time up front shows the family that we care about them and paves the way for cooperation all year. Establishing the sharing of information in this manner also honors a basic fact: the parents have intimate longitudinal information (they know their child over time), while teachers have latitudinal data (they know children at this particular age). Parents are one of teachers' biggest assets. Learning to communicate clearly and effectively will make this relationship more productive.

Frequent two-way communication between parents and teachers builds team support for students. Sending parents a newsletter, packet of information about assignments, report cards, progress reports, or notes to be signed are important, but these are primarily one-way communications—from school to home. Responsive e-mails, texting, phone conferences, and personal contacts throughout the year keep the channels of communication open. The challenge becomes finding time to actively engage parents as colleagues in the education process. If we believe it is really important, we find a way.

Involving parents in classroom activities helps teachers get to know students. How much parents are involved and the kind of help they provide depend on policies of the school, knowledge and skills of the parents, comfort level of the teacher, and the relationship with parents. Some parents can become overbearing. Teachers have to have the courage to make it clear what is appropriate while parents are helping. Taking time to train parent volunteers can help this process immeasurably. It clarifies the expectations while elevating their status as helpers in the classroom.

Keep in mind that parents are sometimes at their wits' end and don't know what to do with a defiant or rebellious child. They hope we will be the fix for their child. In their book, *How to Keep Being a Parent When Your Child Stops Being A Child: A Practical Guide to Parenting Adolescents,* Cooper and McCoy (1999) offer many practical suggestions to help both parents and teachers. During parent conferences, be sure to involve students and to allow time for parents to voice concerns, ask questions, and share their goals for their children.

At some point, it is helpful to ask students to draw a family portrait or a picture of those who live in their house and label the names and relationships of persons illustrated. A variation of this is asking students to draw a floor plan of their house and label the rooms. This provides an opportunity to see who is living in the family unit and how they relate to the student. Many students now come from nontraditional family units, for example, step or blended families, single-parent or multiple-parent situations, and custodial or foster care. For this reason, it is necessary to be cautious when giving this type of assignment. Some students may feel a sense of shame or loss when they describe their family situation. With all children, but especially with younger children, it is important to know their legal guardians, who is the primary caregiver, and who has permission to pick up a child or sign permission slips. In every case, current emergency contacts need to be available not just to the main office but also to the teacher.

BECOMING FAMILIAR WITH CULTURAL PERSPECTIVES

Students from different ethnic backgrounds can present both opportunities and challenges. The culture within which they have been raised (culture of origin) may at times be in conflict with the culture of the community in which they are currently living (culture in place). For teachers, this requires taking time to learn about the cultures within their classroom and school in order to demonstrate sensitivity as well as help with the assimilation of students.

Open discussions with parents can help with this process. It is also best to ask questions of students to gain an understanding of what might be different for them. Sometimes, teachers fear offending people from other cultures by asking them to explain their practices. However, when teachers ask questions with respect and sincerity, they build relationships and can find ways to make learning more relevant for students. This kind of interaction creates safety for students who know that their teachers are interested in knowing their background.

In addition to connecting with parents as described previously, other interventions such as student drawings and responsive journal writing can illuminate cultural perspectives. Labeling items in the classroom in English and a student's native language will help all students learn about languages and build connections for understanding each other.

GETTING TO KNOW STUDENTS' EDUCATIONAL HISTORY

Another aspect of students' identity when they enter a classroom is the history they bring from their previous schooling. Because of dislocations, natural disasters, or other situations, students may have missed months or even years of school. They may have been very successful, earning A's in their classes, or they may have struggled in areas. Either way, it is not enough to just survey their previous report cards to ascertain their abilities or their learning history. How students are graded and assessed is not at all standard, meaning that a student who appears to be struggling may not be a student who doesn't understand. In fact, it may be a student who is bored, who misbehaves in class, or who has other things happening that impact learning.

In a current study on students in alternative education programs, we have made some revealing preliminary discoveries. Most students interviewed indicate that they were doing well in school until some outside event happened that interfered with their ability to focus. This event stole their focus and often went unrecognized by the teachers who were teaching them. Students acknowledge that they quit working, some started fights, while others tried to disappear. In each case, their behavior became the focus, and not the cause of that behavior. They fell off the radar and began to fail, causing them to see themselves as failures and leading to more failure. Some ways to gain an understanding of the impact of their past school history include:

- *Informal survey of parents and previous teachers.* When a student's academic history appears to show signs of difficulty, gaining insight into what has happened can be illuminating. It is essential, however, to listen for the real story. For instance, using open-ended questions will help get the best perspective. Questions such as the following can provide some helpful information:
  - Tell me about Johnny's third-grade year.
  - I noticed that he was absent a lot. What do you know about why that was?
  - What suggestions might you have on how to reach Johnny?
  - What does Johnny enjoy?
  - When was he successful?

The critical aspect of these questions is that they do not lead the respondent to answer in a certain way. This allows previous teachers to share the meaning that they made from Johnny's behavior. Consequently, the astute listener can find clues to understand Johnny's issues as well as what might or might not work well. Listening with an ear for the "open places" is an important way to explore building a relationship that will help Johnny be successful.

Similar conversations with parents can also bring clarity to Johnny's experience in school. Again, it is important not to take comments at face value but to listen to what they may reveal about what Johnny might need or what might work.

- *An educational history interview with students.* We ask students to write down or talk about what they remember from each grade level. For example, if they are in tenth grade, ask what they remember from ninth grade, eighth grade, and so on. It is interesting to note their perceptions of memorable things—rarely anything academic.

It is also helpful to ask struggling students, when did school first start getting hard? In most cases, they will immediately remember what grade level, teacher, and subject where they dropped out mentally. Sometimes, a teacher's remark turned them off. For example, RaShel, a fourth grader, was told by her first-grade teacher that she would never be a good reader. She said she just decided she was dumb and quit trying. Jim, an eleventh grader in an alternative high school program, said he started hating school in third grade when he was embarrassed in front of the class because he didn't know his times tables. He said, "I just didn't care anymore and quit trying." Sometimes, students make a decision based on their perceptions. Andre, a second grader, refused to do any classwork or homework. His teacher was very frustrated and had him checked for learning disabilities. Andre cooperated with all the cognitive assessments and demonstrated there were no learning deficits. When the examiner asked Andre if he was worried about anything, he sat back in his chair, crossed his arms, and said emphatically, "Nope, I decided last year in first grade that the work was too hard, I wasn't gonna do it, and I wasn't gonna worry about it!" Andre had made a decision to avoid doing any work. The examiner was able to coach Andre through some strategies on how to look at his work, identify what parts he understood, what he needed to know, and how to figure out on his own what to do or how to ask for help. He then decided the work really was not that hard. His teacher and his parents were delighted to celebrate Andre's change in mindset that affected his success in school. By getting to know their students, teachers are better equipped to help them learn.

GETTING TO KNOW THEIR TALENTS

An important resource that helps empower learning and teaching within the classroom is recognizing and using the talents of the students. Finding ways to identify these talents among *all* of the students helps to elevate their expertise in various areas, teaches them that they can learn from each other, and builds self-esteem.

- *Student resource posting.* Some teachers prepare a resource bulletin board or, as one teacher called it, an "S-E-T" (skills-expertise-talent) center, where students post their areas of interest and abilities. For example, if someone needs help in math, science, reading, or writing, students see who among their peers were good in those areas and available to provide help. Students also post nonacademic areas of special interest or expertise, for example, guitar, sports, archeology, technology, specific tech games, artistic ability, organizational skills, singing, dancing, and so on. Instead of depending only on the teacher, students begin to regard each other as colearners and share responsibility for developing their learning community. This kind of information gives a different perspective of individual students, builds respect, improves the quality of sharing, and provides opportunities to build relationships.

  Students from different ethnic groups might list things specific to their culture as resources that they may be able to provide. In addition, simply being an "in-class" expert on their culture can build understanding and bridge differences.

- *Talents, interests, and strengths.* There are often students whose talents are well known because of the success they've experienced. It is important to acknowledge these students; however, it is also important to recognize the less-noticed talents of other students. For example, Juan raises sheep. Donald makes and plays the flute. Gwen has a very strong interest in Egyptology. These are important abilities that may not come to light in conventional school activities.

  In a program called Extreme Middle School, piloted at a middle school in Michigan, students were encouraged to do research projects of their choosing, culminating in a presentation to their parents. Among the topics studied were Gustav Mahler, the impact of human behavior on orcas, the aerodynamics of swimming, and the reconstruction of a greenhouse at the school. The students taking on these projects ran the gamut from very talented students to students receiving special education help. No student was denied the opportunity to participate. This indicates the breadth of students' interests and talents at an early age. Tapping into these can be a very important way to make learning relevant to these students.

Teachers usually favor students who participate in class, do assigned work, cooperate, and appear to be "smart." This is a natural reaction because these students affirm teachers' preconceived notion of themselves as good teachers. Focusing on strengths with weaker students can be difficult. Both parents and teachers often focus on mistakes or low grades rather than building on interests and strengths. A positive mindset encourages increased effort and investment in learning for both student and teacher. When we reflect on how it feels when someone gives a compliment, we are much more productive. It is enjoyable to work in an accepting environment.

Sometimes, it is hard to find something good to say about students who are behaving inappropriately or doing unacceptable work. With these students, it is effective to conference individually, like in a writers' or readers' workshop model. Look for opportunities to sit down individually with students, such as "doing lunch with teacher" as a privileged personal time. We encourage teachers to use their creativity to find something positive to say. One way of finding students' strengths is to focus on their interests. This allows teachers to affirm the students' strengths and potentially their work ethic as it pertains to those activities they find interesting. Focusing on effort rather than outcome helps build the growth mindset that leads to a desire for ongoing learning.

- *Mini case studies.* Another way to identify challenging students' strengths is to focus on two or three students for case studies. Doing a mini action-research project will help teachers identify and investigate a question or major issue of concern. The research process then involves (1) identifying the issue, (2) collecting and analyzing data to identify patterns, (3) reflecting on what the data reveal about the students, (4) developing and implementing a plan of action, and (5) evaluating the effectiveness of the plan and what was learned from the process. This format allows teachers to focus on what they are doing and how they can improve (change themselves) to help their students. These case studies can reveal very important data about how the students perceive and process information. Insights gained from doing a case study with one or two students can directly affect the instructional and learning interaction within the whole class.

We all enjoy doing what we are good at, and we tend to avoid what we are not good at doing. While it is necessary to correct errors and misconceptions, focus on only one or two areas at a time. Effective teachers look for opportunities to develop students' assets.

KNOWING OUR LIMITS

"I don't want to know about all their personal problems! I am here to teach mathematics. I want them to leave all that social stuff at the door! They just need to pay attention and do the work!" Ken voiced his frustrations and personal beliefs about his role as a high school teacher. Actually, this perspective is all too common. We are teaching the whole person, not just the intellect. Often the personal issues the students face are obstacles to being able to focus on what is being taught. Learning to balance personal involvement and professional limits is a challenge. This is true of students of all ages. Very often, students can affect us in ways we never thought possible, both positively and negatively. A few guiding principles can help.

1. Let students know you care; don't make them emotionally dependent on you.

2. Empower students to deal with their problems; don't try to fix everything for them.

3. Guide them, believe in them, and encourage them.

4. Recognize your limits; know how to access appropriate resources when needed; don't let students' problems keep you awake at night.

5. Love your students and respect, guide, and encourage them; don't let them manipulate you or sabotage your efforts to teach; know when to maintain boundaries and when to discipline.

6. Remember you are the "alpha" (leader) in the classroom. Be friendly without being a child with the children (or teenager with teens).

CLOSING THOUGHTS

Effective teachers believe all students can learn. They use their knowledge and skills to stimulate cognitive engagement and build trusting relationships with students to enhance learning.

Many students at every age level are dealing with major issues that directly impact their ability to learn, relate to others, and accept our help. Students who have been traumatized by physical or sexual abuse may be too frightened to talk to anyone. What appears to be defiance or disrespect may be manifestations of defense systems for survival. Other issues that affect students' ability to focus and learn include drug and alcohol use by themselves or by their parents; bullying, gang involvement, or other forms of intimidation; and family stressors such as homelessness, divorce, loss of a job, poverty, death of a loved one, natural disasters, military deployment, or involuntary relocation. Students who have a trusting relationship with their teacher will often open up and reveal particulars of their situation. We need the wisdom to know how to listen with respect and caring without being totally overwhelmed and how to access available resources within the community to provide services when needed.

Like most teachers, we entered the profession with idealistic goals of helping every student succeed. We had to learn the hard lesson that we cannot fix problems for our students. When teachers encounter a case where students' needs exceed their resources or ability to help, they need to know how to get professional assistance, and also when to turn loose and let students take responsibility for their choices and actions. In these situations, we keep loving and keep caring, without allowing students to steal our joy or derail our efforts to teach all students effectively. We stay focused on helping those who are willing to work with us. In Chapter 4, we address how to reach students by communicating effectively, dealing with social and behavior issues, and clarifying boundaries needed for a learning community.

Chart 3.1 compares the perspective of teachers who focus on building relationships with the students they teach in a learning classroom with the perspective of teachers in a managed classroom.

Chart 3.1   Perspective on Students in a Learning Classroom vs. a Managed Classroom

Perspective on Students in a Learning Classroom	Perspective on Students in a Managed Classroom
Focus on getting to know students to make teaching and learning relevant for students.	Focus on delivering content with expectation that students take care of their own issues.
Invite students to bring something (interest, experience, questions, wonderings, notices) to the lesson.	Invite students to listen carefully to what they are told and to watch carefully what they are shown.
Accept individual uniqueness of students and what they have to offer.	Regard students as members of class rather than individually unique students.
Look for ways to get to know students through surveys, interviews, resource center, drawings, sharing beautiful thoughts, responsive journal writing, educational history, etc.	Focus on classroom management, control, work completion, grades, and paying attention to what is taught and assigned.
Build on strengths; keep positive attitude.	Point out mistakes and needed corrections.
Get to know families and cultures of students.	Notify parents when there is a problem.
Encourage responsive journal writing with students.	Let students handle their own affairs.
Know your limits and how to access available district and community resources as needed.	Maintain professional distance; make referrals to office as needed.

REFLECTIONS

After reading this chapter, take a few minutes to reflect on the following:

- How well do you know each of your students? How well do you want to know them? What is important to know about them?
- In what ways does knowing your students help you develop a more effective learning community?
- What are some of the obstacles or challenges related to knowing your students?
- Review your own educational history to identify what you remember from each grade level. When and how did you make significant academic decisions or choices?
- What efforts have you made to get to know the family of your students—their culture and the community?
- How do you feel about involving parents in developing your learning community?
- When have you felt yourself being drawn into a students' personal situation that is beyond your control? How did you react? Why did you react that way? What did you do about it?

ACTIONS

- Do student surveys—introductory and advanced.
- Give pre- and posttest of knowledge and skills in content area based on your learning objectives.
- Ask students to draw what school is like for them. Older kids can also write a story, description, or interpretation of their drawings.
- Provide space for resource center of students' skills, expertise, and talents
- Write list in response to question: *What do you need from me and from your classmates to be successful?*
- Ask students to explore their educational history by identifying something memorable from each year of schooling.
- Allow time for responsive student journal writing, take time to read, and respond quickly.
- Do a "beautiful thought" activity to identify what makes your students relax and enjoy something.
- Make personal contact with the family of each student. Document what you learned from the family that helped you know a student and teach more effectively.
- Conduct action research case studies with two or three students to learn from them how they learn.
- Become familiar with district and community resources available for students or families in need.

4

How Do We Reach Our
Students?

*How Procedures and Clear Expectations Develop a
Learning Classroom*

*"Consistency is very important. That means we need to consistently do the
right thing for each student, not the same thing for all students."*

—Nic Cooper

Developing a learning community within a classroom begins with
our relationship with ourselves, that is, understanding who we are
in this process. Next, we need to understand who we are teaching as we
explained in the previous chapter. Now we address specific strategies on
how to create an environment to reach students in a setting that promotes
relationships, relevance, and rigor in learning.

Ben, at one and a half years old, was happily engaged in exploring
the world. Picking up a toy, setting it down, rolling it or throwing it,
everything he did was a new adventure. He laughed at the unexpected
and cried when he hurt himself. He didn't worry about what others
thought; he just was. We wondered how he would appear as a child in
school. Would he still have this sense of wonder? Would he still delight
in learning? How does a little boy like Ben retain this uninhibited desire
to learn? What can teachers do to create the environment that encourages

this exploration? Examine the following scenario where a group of student teachers gathered for a seminar on middle level teaching.

Before the seminar began, Dr. Blodgett made his way around the room, introducing himself to each student and asking them some questions about their goals. When the seminar began, he changed the rock music he'd been playing to something classical and tuned it to barely audible levels. Then he asked the student teachers what they noticed so far. Since he hadn't really presented anything yet, they hesitated. Then one said, "Well, you introduced yourself to each of us."

"OK, and why do you think I did that?"

"To make us feel comfortable and to learn a little about us."

"So, tell me, how might greeting each of you individually impact your attentiveness in this seminar?"

Another student said, "Well, I feel good about being here and am anxious to hear what you have to say."

"Why?"

"Because it seems like you really care about us."

And that was the point of this exercise. Dr. Blodgett wanted the students to feel his acceptance and concern for them when they began the seminar. This modeling allowed them to feel what a student in their classes may feel if they went out of their way to get to know that student a little before teaching him or her.

As experienced teachers, we sometimes take students for granted and feel like we don't need to waste time meeting and greeting, because we have work to do and we will get to know students soon enough based on their behavior, attitude, participation, and grades. However, many educational experts, including Garmston and Wellman (2009; see also www .adaptiveschools.com for more information), advocate "going slow to go fast." They encourage teachers to take the time at the beginning to get to know students and to set up ways to operate so that the classes can be efficient and effective. Wong & Wong (2009) remind us, "Your success during the school year will be determined by what you do on the first days of school" (p. 3). This includes the first moment students enter the classroom, but it's never too late to reflectively evaluate how we can improve our ability to reach students. Today is a good day to start.

Beginning classes with an inclusion activity, one that creates an atmosphere where everyone must participate, helps to reduce fear, and gets students engaged. Such an activity can be used to review the previous day's lesson, build classroom relationships, or learn what students already know about an upcoming topic. It works best when students are paired with different students regularly to avoid cliques and social isolation. Using Kagan & Kagan's cooperative-learning structures (2009) is a good way to make this activity meaningful and engaging for all students. (See www.kaganonline .com for more information.)

Teaching students to collaborate involves teaching effective communication skills. Sometimes we remind teachers, "Hearing is to listening what seeing is to reading." It would never occur to us to say to a student, "You can see, can't you? So read that book." All of the senses have a physical and a mental component. The neurological sensory input of seeing and hearing has to be mentally processed for meaning. Just because students heard what someone said doesn't mean they understood it. Asking open-ended questions encourages students to orally process what they are hearing and thinking without fear of making mistakes. Although discussing communication skills entails writing another whole book, here we want to emphasize that we have to teach some basics about communications to facilitate collaborative learning. For example, instead of "listening with a response running," we encourage students to restate what they heard or to ask clarifying questions. This goes a long way in promoting understanding and preventing misinterpretations. We can reach our students by astutely listening to what they say. When Beth sighs and says that she is not good at writing, when Chuck says that he will never get this, or when Konni gets upset when she does not get an A on her project, we have to ask ourselves, what are they really saying about what they believe, what they feel, or what they fear?

How teachers respond to students in the classroom during discussions provides a powerful way to influence the development of communication skills. For instance, when teachers respond with evaluative responses such as "That's right" or "No, that's wrong," they stifle thinking and keep the focus on outcomes.

In contrast, when teachers listen to the students' responses and comment with "So, you believe . . ."; "Tell me how you arrived at that conclusion"; or "Does anyone see this a different way?" the focus is on the process of thinking. Incidentally, this type of response will encourage others to engage in the discussion. When the focus is on outcomes, students are often unlikely to engage because they may get the answer wrong.

We need to model good listening skills by using eye contact, pausing to reflect on what a student says, and encouraging confident efforts to speak without fear of judgment or criticism. Having open communication creates a learning environment where students feel safe and have the freedom to invest in learning.

In this chapter, we share suggestions for creating a learning environment that are tried and true. Although many of the tips may be familiar to experienced teachers, we include them as a refresher and as a reference for discussion.

THE SETTING—INVITATION TO LEARNING

Consider what students might think in the following scenarios. One classroom appears organized and colorful with desks grouped in pods. The walls display posters with positive messages encouraging students to explore what they notice, think, or wonder. Music is playing. The teacher greets students as they arrive, calling each by name, and welcoming them. In this situation, students quickly settle in, looking forward to what is coming. Another classroom is organized, with desks in straight rows facing the front of the room. Rules and consequences are the only things posted. As students enter, the teacher sits behind a large desk preoccupied with paperwork, ignoring the arrival of students until the bell rings. In this situation, some students will be checked out before the teacher says a word. They will be expecting what they've experienced previously. For the successful student, this may not be a big issue; but for the struggling student, this presents a major obstacle.

To invite students to help create a learning classroom, we encourage teachers to initiate *learning agreements*, which identify behaviors that will help promote learning. They state what is expected. *Rules* usually focus on prohibition of behaviors and punishment for noncompliance rather than encouragement of positive behaviors. Learning agreements state what will help all of the students learn better and prevent many of the issues that interfere with learning.

To create learning agreements that are reflective of the students' needs, we begin by asking the following: What do you need in order to learn? What behaviors will help you be willing to take the risks that are necessary to learn? These questions keep the focus on learning. Then, we encourage brainstorming to make a list. At first, students usually suggest what they think we want to hear. When the students see that we accept their comments without judgment, they begin to trust us enough to be honest and say what they really need. We have to resist the temptation to make suggestions or steer the discussion to what we want the agreement to say. An effective way to make sure every person has a voice is to have each person first make their own personal list of terms and share them with one other person. Then have the pairs meet in small groups to discuss and consolidate their lists before opening the discussion to involve the whole class. As each group shares one or more statements, we write them all down. Then, as a large group, we analyze the statements and condense them to a short list (six to eight items) that we all sign (teacher and students). We did not include a sample here to avoid the temptation to shortcut this process. It is important to review these agreements on a regular basis and update as needed.

Tips for Classroom Organization

The physical arrangement of a classroom directly affects how it functions. Items displayed identify what is important. To keep the focus on learning, we encourage teachers to use the environment to clearly communicate how students can be successful. Here are some suggestions:

- Clearly display key strategies students need to know and use throughout the school year, for example, reminders about safety, interactions, collaboration, problem-solving strategies, overcoming obstacles, and principles to nurture caring for each other.

- Display assignments and day's agenda in same conspicuous place.
- Provide easy access to needed materials and resources.
- Identify marked places for returned work, turned in assignments, and warm-up or do-now activities when students enter the classroom.
- Establish areas for comfortable reading, computer work, research, and quiet study.
- Display student class work and artwork and include place for students to post items of interest about themselves or their activities.
- Post lists of "my job for the day" to involve students in classroom functions.
- Create a display of the teacher's family or interests as a way of helping students feel more connected to the teacher.

Overall, students should feel like they belong, know what to expect, and have access to what is needed. The schedules, meaningful displays, consistent procedures and routines, availability of information and resources, and arrangement of furniture are all coordinated to give students a sense of security and confidence that facilitates learning.

Emergency Procedures

Every school has action plans for safely getting students out of harm's way in case of fire, severe weather, or a dangerous intruder. These procedures should be clearly stated and practiced. Include a way to keep track of students and a way to communicate in case a dangerous situation presents itself. Teachers can enhance the effectiveness of these exercises by making sure students understand the importance of doing exactly what is asked and taking the task seriously. Being quiet during a drill, for example, is often seen as an optional thing. However, this is critical since communicating in an emergency requires that all can hear and follow instructions immediately.

Novelty as a Tool to Reach Students

Our brains search for novelty. Without it, students tend to become passive or bored and often resort of doodling, talking with neighbors, daydreaming, or creating commotion. Since students' disengagement appears to be disinterest or lack of motivation, teachers are apt to scold or lecture about the need to pay attention. Here are a few suggestions on ways to use novelty to stimulate engagement in a learning classroom:

- Acting out stories or events, doing role playing, or dressing up like historical or literary characters.

- Rearranging the room, seating charts, or normal sequence of events.
- Using music, popular and classical (Kagan produces CDs for classrooms) for setting a mood; creating lyrics, raps, rhythms to remember information.
- Using color to create a brain-friendly environment. Some research indicates that earth tones (brown, green, blue, purple) facilitate memory. Reds, yellows, and oranges are good for emphasis. Mixing color can also facilitate remembering information presented in lists.
- Modifying lighting by using lamps and/or by using colored crepe paper over fluorescent lights to create a less harshly lit environment.
- Designing lessons based on real-life problems or projects; bringing in outside resources or surprise visitors.
- Organizing "mock" themes; for example, include a theme based on the television show *Crime Scene Investigation (CSI)* for a math or science lesson, demonstrate a new concept as if introduced on a different planet, put an idea on trial.
- Using games to develop skills related to the content; inviting students to create games based on the lesson.
- Changing pace of instruction and giving choices in ways to demonstrate understanding, for example, oral presentation, research report, multimedia production, interactive project, graphic design, interpretive dance, activity to engage others, applied outcome, illustrations, musical rendition.
- Diversifying instructional methods, for example, large small group lessons, cooperative learning, lecture or direct instruction, project learning, experimental challenges, modeling, Socratic questioning, independent or group research, self-paced lessons.

Time-Savers to Maximize Instruction

The efficient use of time is another important aspect of reaching students in a learning classroom. Some simple procedures can literally conserve hours of instructional time, create a safer environment, avoid disturbances, and minimize hurtful conditions. Consider these situations:

Mr. Kennedy shuffles through his papers and waits for students to get their books and materials out. About seven minutes have passed before he stands in front of the class and lectures. About halfway through the period, he says, "OK, class we will begin the discussion on the causes of the Civil War. Find a partner and discuss some of the reasons why the Civil War began." Students randomly mill around the room, some find partners while others stay seated and avoid eye contact. The transition from instruction to discussion takes five minutes or more. There is no system for putting partners together, and the broad instructions do not challenge students to invest in their own learning. Without realizing it, Mr. Kennedy also set up a situation for students to be excluded. Social isolation can be particularly painful for less popular students.

Ms. Edwards begins instruction immediately and after a brief lecture on the Civil War, says, "OK, now get with your three-o'clock partner and answer these two questions: What might be some reasons that slavery was so important to the South? What might have been different if the Civil War had ended with the South winning? Be prepared to share your partner's thoughts." Within thirty seconds, all students have partners and are engaged in focused discussion. Ms. Edwards started class immediately, used an established system for partnering, and asked specific questions with expected accountability for sharing what was discussed. She used one of our suggested time-saving procedures for partnering like those listed as follows.

Set up "o'clock partners" as a practical way to establish a community feeling and expedite partnering activities. At the beginning of the year, students are given a sheet of paper with a clock face and a list of getting-to-know-you prompts, such as "describe your favorite place to visit," or "list three things you would do with a million dollars." The students are instructed to mingle, often to music, and stop when the music stops, picking a nearby partner. Each student enters the other person's name at the one-o'clock position on partner's sheet and shares his or her answer to a prompt. After a few minutes, the music starts and the process is repeated. Within a short time, each student has twelve potential partners for pairing activities. Later, for partner activities, the teacher only needs to say, go to your five-o'clock partner (or other time position), and all students know who their partner is. No one is left sitting alone in the process.

Establish an attention first signal such as chimes, bells, rhythmic hand-claps, or a hand gesture. This is a way of getting students' attention without shouting. Simply saying "please pause" in a firm clear voice can also work. *Whatever the chosen signal, it needs to be practiced and consistently used.*

Use a random system for calling on students instead of just calling on those with raised hands, so all students are engaged and accountable for participation. This minimizes delays waiting for students to respond.

Use a visible timer to help students stay focused and complete tasks at a reasonable pace. Encourage students to systematically set up their own timelines and deadlines for completing work.

Maximize efficiency by creating an environment where students are willing to take risks and share what they are honestly thinking without fear of embarrassment if they make a mistake. Encourage students to confidently explain what part of the information they do understand and to ask for clarification of what they need to know.

Differentiate assignments to encourage independent work for those who can go ahead on their own. This provides more time to help those who are struggling without delaying those who don't need the extra help.

Take "brain breaks." Practice using brief intermissions to physically stretch, tell a joke, or move and then immediately refocus. Doing this actually stimulates cognitive engagement and makes more productive use of time.

Invest time on essentials. Instead of trying to cover every page of every textbook, analyze curriculum to make sure students know what is important. Spend time on what matters.

Establish routines to minimize interruptions, for example, when to get supplies, where to hand in papers, where to pick up assignments, what to do with late work, when and how to access the bathroom pass, or when and how to sharpen pencils or get Kleenex.

Build a repertoire of short stimulators to use when there are moments between activities. These can be Jeopardy-type quizzes, puzzlers, trivia-type questions related to content, "quick writes," brain games, activity sheets, short stories, rhythms and rhymes, and so forth, which are fun and easily accessed.

Be prepared. Careful planning eliminates wasted time and energy for you and for the students. Making students wait while we get things together is disrespectful of their time and opens the door for disengagement. Be punctual in starting and finishing class to maximize time.

REACHING THE DIFFICULT STUDENT

A guiding principle to use when dealing with difficult or disruptive behavior is that *there's always a reason, but there's never an excuse.* Recognizing there is a reason and addressing it without excusing the behavior helps teach students how to succeed and avoids making them victims. Earlier, we mentioned that anger, when directed at another person, is typically connected to feelings of hurt or fear. So when Jim enters a classroom, assumes a defiant posture, and dares the teacher to engage him, the apparent anger is actually a defensive reaction to some hurt or fear he is experiencing.

In the classroom, there may be students who appear to be disengaged and disrespectful, who disrupt learning for others and resist it themselves. We can find these students exasperating. Sometimes they can even be disabling to us when we are teaching a lesson and are interrupted by their misbehavior. It is frustrating and can also be somewhat humiliating when their intention appears to embarrass us.

A critical factor in positively impacting these situations is to frame them in a manner that helps build understanding and promotes a positive outcome. To do this, we need to again return to the idea of forming relationships with our students while having a deep understanding of ourselves. These situations become disabling when teachers take the students' behavior personally. When trapped in the lizard brain, teachers are apt to lash out, focused on punishing the student and gaining control of the situation. It feels like a fight for survival.

To reframe this situation, we need to believe that we have the power and that we will keep it. We have it; the students do not. Power struggles only happen if we are willing to struggle. We are more inclined to struggle if we fear we may lose power. Now, this doesn't mean that teachers are tyrants. It means that structure brings safety. Boundaries let students know what behavior is appropriate and what behaviors make them successful. Blame and shame play no part in discipline. Blame simply sidesteps the real issues. Shame in fact is the greatest growth inhibitor.

So, we need to slow ourselves down and look for reasons. On occasion, we may feel that students are just trying to get attention. For some, this means to ignore them because we certainly don't want to give them something that they want when they are asserting themselves in negative ways.

It is best to rethink this. Instead of considering it an either/or situation, perhaps it's a matter of meeting their need by using the opportunity to teach more appropriate behavior. It is a little counterintuitive to respond to a pathological need for attention by outright denying it and expecting that to change the need. It is much more likely to accelerate or amplify the behavior. And do we really know why they have this need? So, another solution is to recognize the need but respond to it by finding its cause, thereby meeting the need for attention.

Darryl constantly makes side comments, playing for laughs at the expense of Ms. Cheng. His comments border on the inappropriate as they refer to her appearance, her knowledge, or the importance of what she is saying. Ms. Cheng hears the comments and feels the hurt that it appears they are intended to cause. This is where things can either go in a positive or negative direction. If Ms. Cheng responds to the hurt by hurting back—a common response described as "hurt people hurt people"—she will set in motion a cycle where she will ultimately lose control. She is acceding to a power struggle by accepting Darryl's mode of interaction and attempting to outdo him. On the other hand, if she recognizes the hurt but then pauses and also recognizes that this isn't really personal but related to some hurt Darryl is feeling, she will have the opportunity to react differently.

She hears the comment about "how stupid this discussion is" and moves in Darryl's direction. She pauses and asks the students to engage in a quick-write reflection on the topic they are discussing. With that break in the discussion, she kneels next to Darryl and asks him to join her away from the other students.

In a calm firm voice, she states, "Darryl, I have been hearing your comments and have been distracted at times. I am concerned because it appears that you are more focused on drawing attention to yourself than engaged in the learning. I want to help you be successful, so I need to have a better understanding of what is impacting you that you feel the need to behave this way. I am going to want to sit down with you and discuss this after class. In the meantime, I want you to do your writing on what is hurting you or upsetting you that causes you to need to disrupt class."

This conversation takes place quickly, away from the other students, and at this point is one-way. The goal here is to acknowledge Darryl's need for attention by giving it to him, but on the teacher's terms. The second goal is to reframe the behavior as a response to something else, instead of an attack on the teacher, or as either rude or inconsiderate (potentially shaming terms).

Darryl is being held accountable but not shamed. His need for attention is being addressed but in a manner that will give the teacher important information. He is learning that there will be no power struggles here. He is also learning that his teacher cares about what is really going on.

In interviews with students in alternative programs, we have heard them describe how they misbehaved in school because they didn't care anymore. With further exploration, it is clear they didn't begin that way but that something external to school may have interfered with their desire to learn. On occasion, it is failure in school, but more often, it is trauma outside of school that preoccupies them, making lessons in reading, writing, and arithmetic less than compelling. Teachers who harshly dealt with their behavior became another part of the problem.

> It is not about lowering the standard; it is about helping them to see the doable route to achieving the standard.

What is unfortunate, however, is that these students were truly saying "Notice me!" but in the same manner that a drowning person says "Help me!" Teachers who were threatened by students' behavior, however, heard "I'm out to get you!" and reacted to defend themselves. They didn't take time to learn what might have been behind this behavior so they might have been able to intervene.

It's also important to remember the following principle: *there is never an excuse*. This pertains to two aspects of these interactions. *First,* the students may never be allowed to feel that their misbehavior is acceptable because they have difficulties in their lives. We may understand why they behave in the manner that they do, but we cannot condone it or ignore it. To do so makes them victims. Labeling them victims disables them and excuses their failures. We cannot do that! The *second* aspect of this principle is that we cannot alter the expectations or lower the bar to make it appear that they succeeded when in fact they didn't. It is not about lowering the standard; it is about helping them to see the doable route to achieving the standard.

We cannot change their home situations, but we can understand the students and guide them. Our goal is to guide them over the hurdles that all successful students must attain.

Consistency is often a focus when asking teachers the key to good classroom discipline. We would agree with this caveat. Consistency means to "consistently do what is right for each student." It does not mean doing the same thing for all students.

So, when we relax, learn about our students, identify the behavior that needs to be changed, and do what is necessary to help them change it by teaching them better ways, we successfully maintain a learning focus and build quality relationships. We control a variable to help them succeed.

Another suggestion, grounded in brain research, is to do the unexpected. As we've noted, behavior has a reason. Students who disrupt or disengage are telling us something. They also have experience with this behavior. It feels normal to them. Consequently, they also have a pretty good idea of the response that it will elicit. This is where we can throw them a curve that will get their attention. Instead of a well-meaning and probably well-worded lecture, one they have undoubtedly heard previously in some form, we need to do something different. Our brains sort incoming information on the basis of novelty and threat. Predictable behavior is not novel and will not typically constitute a threat. Unpredictable behavior, something that is unexpected, however, will be novel and will likely be more favorably considered.

In Ms. Cheng's example earlier, it is likely that Darryl expected to be yelled at and told he was rude and to "behave, or else . . . ." He was likely primed for an argument and ready to put his teacher on the defensive. It had worked before. What happened though was different. She described his behavior and its impact, but instead of engaging him in a discussion that may have become an argument at that moment, she demonstrated concern for him. She kept control of the situation but redirected it to learn more about Darryl. It is unlikely that Darryl experienced that previously.

A subtle part of Ms. Cheng's intervention was to give Darryl a different writing assignment. Since the other students were writing at the time, his different task would be between the two of them. He was being respected in this way. It demonstrated that Ms. Cheng valued a relationship with him. When teachers understand that the behavior is not about them, it allows them to feel less threatened and to become an investigator. Like in *CSI*, there is a crime here. The crime is "not learning"; the teacher's job is to solve it.

Students who struggle develop ways of surviving that often conflict with desired classroom behavior. Their lack of success is frustrating but cannot discourage us. Here are some key things to remember:

1. Know your hot buttons.

2. Learn to read students' behavior.

3. Search for the anchoring incidents that color their perspective.

4. Honor the goals of their behavior while maintaining control of the situation (ignoring a student seeking attention is counterintuitive, but give the attention on your terms).

5. Listen attentively to see the world from their perspective.

6. Know their interests and honor them.

7. Help them learn to help themselves and to help others.

8. Be consistent, meaning consistently do what is right for each student.

9. Admit mistakes.

10. Demand accountability but refuse to shame.

11. Work hard to help them succeed while being aware of the need to foster independence and self-efficacy.

When we can remember these behaviors, we will have a greater chance of building relationships with students who seemingly resist us. We will be showing them respect on a deep level while expecting it also.

Difficult students' inappropriate behaviors can often give rise to conflicts among peers. Conflicts are inevitable and need to be welcomed. This is not exactly what many would like to hear, but it is the truth. Conflicts, however, need not be destructive. They become destructive when they are avoided.

Embracing conflict, in contrast, can empower good communication and bring those with differing views closer. Here are some important points about conflicts:

- They are normal, natural, and healthy.
- In order to solve a conflict, we need to understand the other person.
- In order to understand the other person, we need to accept him or her.
- In order to solve a conflict, we need to keep our focus on the real goal and not just winning the argument.
- Conflicts are usually a perception of mutually exclusive needs.

When conflict is accepted as normal, natural, and healthy, it reduces the fear associated with it. We need not fear it; we just need to work to understand where the differences are. When well utilized, conflict brings people together because it promotes understanding others who could be a critical resource to solving a problem. We may need them to figure it out! Therefore, we cannot afford to make them the villain, which could keep us from reaching a solution.

Resolving a conflict is not about winning an argument; it is about reaching an understanding and agreeing on a course of action. Sometimes, when we are in conflicts with others, we get so focused on winning that we forget what the real goal was.

With students, there is also the issue of perceived loss of power on the part of the adult. This can seriously inhibit good communication. No matter who is the person in authority, the need to understand each other's perspective is critical. Often this needs to be first established by the adult. Then the student can follow. Notice how that might work in this situation:

Mr. Wilcox notices Robert's head down while he was giving an assignment.

"Robert, did you understand the assignment?"

"Sure," Robert answers flippantly.

"OK, tell me what is expected then."

"You want us to do something for tomorrow," Robert says with a mocking grin.

"OK, we'll need to clarify this after class, Robert." Mr. Wilcox then finishes the class, summarizes what was taught, and dismisses the students.

He catches Robert before he leaves and says, "OK Robert, tell me what's up."

"What do you mean? Nothing's up."

"You seem angry, and I want to know what's going on with you so I can understand you better."

Robert sighs and says, "Nothing's going on. I'm just bored."

"Bored? Tell me more."

"I hate this stuff."

"OK, what is it that you hate? I'm not sure I understand."

"I hate all the reading you make us do."

"I see. So, when I assign reading, you feel frustrated and tune out."

"Yep, that's about it."

"Tell me more about why reading is an issue."

"Just don't like it."

"OK, so it's difficult for you?"

"No, I just don't like it. I can read OK, just don't like to do it."

"I don't understand. Tell me what it is about reading that you don't like?"

"Look, I don't have time for it, OK?"

"OK, so the problem is you need more time to do the reading, and I need you to do it to keep up with the discussion. Is that right?"

"Yeah, I guess. There's no way I can get enough time to myself at home to finish all you want us to do. So, I come to class unprepared and feel stupid."

"And then you end up not trying and failing."

"Exactly. It's the story of my life."

"OK—so how can we change this? I mean, I need you to keep up with this work, and I also want you to stop giving up. What would help?"

"Not give me any homework?"

"Hmm—doesn't seem like that helps you keep up. Is it hard to work at home every night?"

"Not every night. Usually my parents aren't home on Wednesday night and one weekend night. Those times I can work OK."

"So how about I give you the assignments ahead of time so you can work on them when you can focus instead of the night before they are due. Would you do them if you had that consideration?"

"Yeah, that would work OK."

"Good, I'll do that then."

In this conversation, Mr. Wilcox resisted asserting the power difference when Robert was initially insolent in his responses. By not taking that bait, he actually maintained control of the situation and brought it to a resolution that likely improved their feelings about each other. Resisting the power struggle that Robert was setting up teaches an important lesson. *When teachers engage in power struggles, they are saying that there is power to be struggled over.* By resisting that setup, Mr. Wilcox, in contrast, said, "There is no need for a struggle here—I have the power and you don't." Having said that, he didn't need to panic and try to overpower Robert; he could listen respectfully and discover a solution that met both of their needs.

BUILDING ALTERNATIVE APPROACHES

There are times when students just don't fit the conventional school setting. At times, the assumption is made that this is due to a lack of intelligence, motivation, or effort. Other times, their home lives are seen as the reason for their struggles. In any case, these students can and will succeed if their needs are understood and the right type of programs are developed.

One problem, however, is that school officials are often pressed into doing what is expeditious and not what makes sense. Expeditious solutions for struggling students focus on (1) removing them from the general population to minimize the impact of their problematic behavior, (2) setting the bar lower so that they can appear to succeed, (3) assigning the lower seniority or less capable teachers to teach them, and (4) being unconcerned about the real success of the program and more concerned about not being bothered by these students. These types of programs are often placed in settings that are not being used for anything else and may be only marginally suitable for teaching. They typically use programmed learning with computers or worksheets, marking progress by the completion of modules. Too often, they allow students the freedom to break rules that are not acceptable in other settings (smoking being the predominant one, but also the freedom to leave campus) and usually have staff who address students informally and dress down for their students. Unfortunately, these programs do little to improve learning. They also do little to inform the schooling systems about what they may change to address the needs of students falling through the cracks.

The remedy for this is to make the primary focus on improving learning instead of removing the problem or making it less visible. When learning is the focus, then programs are designed to respond to the varied needs of the students, attending to the research that suggests what supports help build resilience. Also, valid and reliable tools must be used to evaluate the programs in order to see what works, so it can be generalized to others. Programs that work for struggling students often include elements that can and should be available to all students. The system that collects, analyzes, and applies the data from these alternative programs, then, will improve overall. Some of the elements that work with struggling students are:

1. Creative teaching strategies that speak to varied learning modalities

2. Teachers who believe they will succeed and who will push the students

3. A service component where students learn to focus on others

4. A mentoring component where students are encouraged by meaningful adults who support them, guide them, and also expect them to succeed

5. A team building, or community aspect, that encourages students to form relationships with each other and support each other

6. A systematic evaluation of the program that includes modifying the program to meet the varied needs of students

Although some younger teachers may be successful working with these students, they also need to be mentored to avoid feeling they have to be friends on the students' level to relate to them. Excellent, experienced teachers with a history of building high quality relationships with students are ideal for this situation. However, the system that typically exists rewards the best teachers with the students who present the least challenge. If the goal is to help students to succeed, that thinking needs to change.

Students who are exposed to alternative approaches that make sense also learn that they count. Students who are being "warehoused" know it and know that they are being discarded.

CLOSING THOUGHTS

Reaching students relies on knowing them as well as on teachers knowing themselves. In addition to responding to inappropriate behaviors, it also means setting the stage so that there is less likelihood that these behaviors will present themselves. Engaged students, who are wondering what will happen next, are less likely to be bored. Respected students, who know that they will be heard, are less likely to engage in behaviors that shout for attention. Clear and fair expectations that are collaboratively designed will help students know what is expected of them. Teaching and modeling appropriate skills emphasizes what is important and will greatly increase the likelihood that they will be exhibited. Chart 4.1 summarizes what this would look like in a learning classroom and a managed classroom.

Chart 4.1   Reaching Students in a Learning Classroom vs. a Managed Classroom

Reaching Students in a Learning Classroom	*Reaching Students in a Managed Classroom*
Focus on learning who each student is and establishing positive relationships.	Focus on responding to behaviors without consideration for what the student brings.
Collaborate with students to design classroom norms for interaction and behaviors.	Dictate rules and regulations with consequences to maintain discipline.
Focus on creating an environment that communicates an expectation to explore and learn.	Focus on creating an environment that is primarily controlled and orderly.
Establish clear expectations for the classroom and take the time to teach the necessary skills to make it work.	Establish rules to maintain order; expect students to know how to behave.
Encourage collaboration with structured processes to keep all students engaged.	Place the emphasis on individual work or group work without clear processes to keep all engaged.
Notice struggling learners with a focus on understanding the cause of their struggles.	Notice struggling learners with a focus on getting them to finish assignments.
Recognize when a student upsets you and engaging in reflection to determine the cause.	Recognize when a student upsets you and focusing on controlling that student's behavior.
Paraphrase and clarifying the students' responses and focusing on thinking and encouraging active listening.	Evaluate responses according to the teacher's goals and focusing on the right outcomes.
Embrace conflict and work with the student to understand each other's perspectives.	Avoid conflict or use it to exert power over the student to assert authority.

REFLECTIONS

After reading this chapter, take a few minutes to reflect on the following:

- Considering what you have learned about your students, what might it tell you about how to respond to them?
- Thinking about those students who trouble you most, what do you need to understand in order to assist them in the learning process?

- What processes have you established to create a safe environment in your classroom? What processes might you need to change?
- When you think of your classroom setting, in what ways might it encourage safety and learning? In what ways might it be limiting?
- How do you teach your students appropriate communication skills? How might you make this a part of your future classes?
- When you face a conflict, what emotions do you experience? How do these emotions impact your responses?
- Reflect on your classroom setting. What might a student notice when entering your classroom? How will this perception enhance safety and promote learning?
- Think about a classroom in which you felt a sense of comfort when you entered it. What about that classroom made you feel that way?
- Think about your use of time in your classroom. Where do you lose time from instruction by not having preestablished procedures?
- Think of a class where you were asked to find a partner. How did you feel when this was left to chance?

ACTIONS

- Identify a student who troubles you and list what you know about him or her.
- Reflect on how you feel in the presence of this student and students like him or her. What does this tell you about your own perspective, fears, or hurts?
- Practice paraphrasing other people who are discussing something with you. Remember to keep it brief and focus on the essence of their thought. Notice what happens in the conversation.
- Practice pausing before responding when in a conflict with someone, giving yourself time to reflect on what you want to say. Notice how this might impact the conversation.
- Reflect on a time when you collaborated with another person to solve a problem or create something. What happened? What can you learn from that experience?
- Identify colleagues whose classrooms are highly organized. Visit them and notice what students' needs they took into account when organizing their classrooms. Ask questions to discern how they made the decisions they made.
- Pick an "attention first" signal and try it in your classroom. Remember to practice it and to frame it as a respectful way to get students' attention.

5

How Do We Teach Our Students?

How to Engage Students in Their Own Learning With Rigor and Relevance

"Learning is created by the learner."

—*Betty K. Garner*

"What do you see?" Andy, an experienced seventh-grade teacher, asked his students after attending a seminar on teaching and reaching students. This was the first day of a unit on ancient civilizations, and he was experimenting with an approach he learned about in the seminar. He had posted an assortment of pictures around of the room. One student said, "I see a bunch of pictures about Egypt, Rome, Greece, Mayan, or Inca stuff." The others sat passively waiting for the teacher to start "teaching." Andy had seen this behavior all too often. He was unsure if this new approach would work. After waiting a few minutes with no response, he invited students to get up and look more closely at all the pictures.

He asked, "What do you notice?" At first, one or two students would point to something and say, "Is this what you want us to see?" Others milled around, glancing superficially at the pictures and at Andy to see if they were done. Andy had to resist the temptation to point out various items of interest.

He again asked, "What do you notice as you look at the pictures?" He added, "What questions come to mind? What do you wonder about?"

Several students looked at him as if he had three heads. "What do you mean 'what questions'?" one asked. In a moment of insight, Andy realized that he usually asked the students for answers. When he did ask, "Any questions?" at the end of a lesson, it was more rhetorical (since they rarely asked anything).

Andy waited patiently. Gradually, students started noticing details, comparing one picture to another and becoming little detectives to identify interesting things they were noticing. Some even started asking each other "wondering" questions like "I wonder what they would have done if . . . ?" When Andy called them back together for a group discussion, the students were eager to share interesting things they had noticed. A few students openly asked questions such as "Why did they . . . ?"; "How did they . . . ?"; "What were the causes . . . ?"; "When did this . . . ?"; "I wondered if . . . ?" Andy was thrilled with the students' participation. It was like they had an awakening. The students' input provided multiple connections for the new concepts he would be presenting throughout the lesson.

When we use an approach like this, we invite students to bring something to the lesson instead of telling them everything. We stimulate their cognitive engagement and encourage them to trust their own abilities to gather, organize, and process information for meaning. They provide the connections we need to make the instruction relevant to their own lives. We become colearners with the students. How we teach students directly impacts how they benefit from what we teach. In an interview conducted by Haffar (2009), Duckworth stated, "I believe that to teach about any subject matter, we need to give the students the subject matter, not words about the subject matter." When we make a simple change such as starting lessons by showing some artifacts, pictures, writings, or diagrams related to the concept and asking students what they see (sensory input, seeing with their eyes) and what they notice (interpretations, seeing with their minds), we encourage them to invest in their own learning.

It has been our experience that students often become mentally disengaged in their learning when they are bored (already know what we are teaching), they don't believe they need to know what we are presenting (info appears irrelevant to them), they are not challenged (info lacks rigor), or they don't understand (don't have a clue what we are teaching).

We normally see kindergarteners come to school full of curiosity and excitement to learn, asking lots of questions and willing to try most anything. Too often, by the time they get to second or third grade, they are conditioned to focus on getting the right answer to the teachers' questions instead of asking questions. Billy, a fourth grader said, "I would rather get an F than ask a question." Older students who are struggling in school become experts at evasive maneuvers to avoid work or get the teacher off track. Tim, a forty-five-year-old man who had graduated from high school without being able to read, asked for private instructions after going through a divorce because he no longer had his wife to take care of shopping, paying bills, and reading directions. He described what it was like for him in middle and high school. He smiled mischievously as he said, "I didn't understand what the teacher was talking about and couldn't do the work, so every day I came with a plan. I gave the teacher ten minutes; the rest was mine!" Students like Tim are often a mystery. We wonder why they are such troublemakers and resist our efforts to help them. Tim was able to memorize enough information to get by with oral testing and cheating. His teachers were frustrated and let him squeak by with minimal grades just to keep him in school and out of their particular class. He was one of many who fall through the cracks of the educational system.

What happens when you ask students "What do you notice?" and "What do you wonder about?"

1. They focus attention and gather more sensory data. Teacher sees what they see.

2. Their curiosity is aroused and they become investigators.

3. They discern details (usually more than what teacher notices) and determine relevance.

4. They make connections with prior knowledge and experience.

5. They help the teacher identify their existing vocabulary and interests related to the topic.

6. They are set free from guessing what the teacher wants them to say.

7. They are empowered to trust themselves and their own capabilities.

8. They respond to teacher's endorsement of their abilities.

9. They build trusting relationship with teacher.

10. They are freed from fear of making mistakes, because there is no *one* right answer.

11. Teacher encourages originality, creativity, personal investment, and emotional involvement.

12. Instead of trying to motivate, teacher accesses students' natural interest in new things.

13. Students open up with their wonderings and questions—without the invitation, they wait passively for the teacher to tell them information.

14. They are doing the work; they become their own teachers; the teacher facilitates learning.

> Rigor involves more than content. It also involves character traits of effort, persistence, and commitment based on a need to know on the part of students and teachers.

We enjoy teaching students of all ages when they are cooperative and successful. We have more difficulty with students who just don't get it despite our efforts to adapt to their learning styles, modify activities and assignments, review repeatedly, vary modalities, and provide extra tutoring or support. Rigorous standards are wonderful guides; however, the reality is a large number of students come to us without the basic knowledge and skills they need to meet those standards. Rigor involves more than content. It also involves character traits of effort, persistence, and commitment based on a need to know on the part of students and teachers. We encourage teachers to assess their personal assets, to reexamine their basic beliefs about teaching and learning, and to get to know their students, so they can build trusting relationships and make learning relevant.

DECIDING HOW TO TEACH

One of our biggest challenges is deciding *how* to teach a specific concept to specific students in a way that the information is relevant and rigorous. State requirements and district curriculum mandate *what* to teach. Common Core Standards along with 21st century skills and an abundance of educational materials identify what students "should know and be able to do." However, we still have considerable freedom in choosing how we teach. This provides opportunities for creativity and personal preferences within the context of a structured educational system.

Despite this freedom and the availability of extensive research on effective teaching, many teachers still choose to teach the way they were taught. In our preservice classes, we ask aspiring teachers to close their eyes and visualize themselves teaching. Smiles spread across their faces as they see themselves fulfilling their dreams as a teacher. When asked to share what they saw in their minds, many saw themselves in front of a classroom presenting an interesting lesson to well-behaved students who were eager to learn. Since the majority of those who become teachers were good in school, they simply assume, often on an intuitive level, what worked for them would work for their students. Even though many teachers say this is not true, we observe this to be the case as we work with experienced teachers across the country. We notice a disconnect between theory (what teachers say they believe) and practice (what they actually do in the classroom). The myth of teacher as the dispenser of knowledge still permeates practice.

Beliefs Affect How We Teach

If we believe the teacher's job is transmission of information, we do our best to clearly explain new concepts, give lots of practice, and test students' ability to show what they remember from the lesson. We work very hard to make sure students follow directions, complete assignments, and score well on tests. If students don't do well, we go over the information again hoping it sticks. Without realizing, we can be so intent on helping students get correct responses and good grades that we literally turn off their natural curiosity by spoon feeding them information bit by bit and making them totally dependent on us.

If we believe every student can learn, we make every effort to provide access to success through adaptations in methods, materials, resources, levels of difficulty, complexity, pacing, and types of information. Within every classroom, the capabilities, knowledge, intelligence, talents, and skills of students are as varied as their

> *Creativity becomes a teacher's primary resource to meet the needs of each student while taking into consideration the needs of all as a group.*

personalities, motivation, effort, interests, beliefs, backgrounds, and experiences. In addition to the normal variations among students, teachers also have to meet the needs of learning disabled students. Creativity becomes a teacher's primary resource to meet the needs of each student while taking into consideration the needs of all as a group. Our role becomes that of a coach or facilitator. We can provide information, model what to do, encourage thinking, supply resources, assess understanding, provide opportunities to practice, and apply what is taught, but the students are the only ones who can process information for meaning and make it their own. Too often, we do much more work than the students (Jackson, 2009).

Alex uses a metaphor to help his students understand their responsibility for learning. When he encounters students who are unmotivated or totally turned off to school, he asks them if they have a favorite restaurant. Most respond without hesitation, although some can't decide among several favorites. Alex then asks them to describe how they sit down at a table and order their food. Before long, the students are getting hungry as they picture their favorite meal being prepared for them. He then asks, "What would you do if the server brought the food and shoved it in your mouth?"

Reactions vary from being repulsed and politely resisting to angrily spitting the food out or shoving it right back at the server with loud protests. Alex goes on to explain, "The teacher is like the server. As a teacher, I can prepare and present the 'food,' but I can no more shove information into your head than the server can shove food into your mouth."

He pauses for students to reflect then asks, "What do you understand by this?" Someone says, "You mean I have to teach myself?" Alex found that lecturing about the importance of taking responsibility for learning or getting motivated has little effect. Using a short example like this quickly brings home the point.

If we believe learning is created by learners, our job is to equip them with the cognitive tools to make sense of unfamiliar information, so they truly become self-directed, life-long learners. Learning theories are many and varied. The best way to learn about learning is to keep up with current research and to become a researcher. When we engage students as researchers to think about their own thinking, we reactivate how they learned before starting school.

From day one, infants start to build a mental database through sensory input, observing, listening, tasting, touching, and smelling. With our students' immersion in media overload, they are constantly bombarded with external stimulation and internal mental noise that interferes with focus. They often use what we call blurred and sweeping perception—they see and hear without processing. Every scientist knows that a key skill in any experiment is astute observation and collection of data. In school, students might perceive the teachers' voice or presentation as irrelevant background noise rather than the focus of attention they need to input the information. Sometimes, we literally have to teach students to become aware of what their senses are telling their brains. Encouraging them to reflect and ask themselves what they see and what they notice help them begin to trust their own abilities to gather and process information.

Teach the Way They Learn

As babies become aware of their senses, they begin to imitate what they see and hear, starting with sounds, gestures, and facial expressions. This is a normal way of learning that continues through life. When learning something new, we generally imitate someone who knows about what we want to learn. For example, to learn a musical instrument, we imitate someone who knows how to play it; to learn a sport, we imitate the coach or other players. Starting school, we imitate the teacher writing letters or doing math problems. Later in school, we continue to imitate the teacher as information and exercises become more complex. The problem comes if we stop at imitation and never make the information or process our own. For example, if we demonstrate how to divide fractions and give the students a series of problems to work that are very similar to the model, they may be able to imitate the procedure and get correct answers. However, if we slightly change the level of complexity or give them a word problem where they have to set up a problem using divisions of fractions, they are lost because they did not really understand the operation; they just imitated the steps. It is much more effective to do fewer problems and have students explain how and why they did it the way they did, so we can see their thinking, diagnose misconceptions, and clarify for understanding.

As children grow and develop, they quickly begin to experiment. Their curiosity reaches out to everything around them as they playfully discover their ability to make things happen, noticing cause–effect relationships, developing a sense of agency, and expanding their database with every situation. In school, this natural curiosity is often stifled within the structure of regimented lessons. Using manipulatives in mathematics, for example, gives students the opportunity to physically interact with materials to learn about quantity, spatial relationships, shapes, size, measurements, and operations in a concrete situation before going to abstract numeric or symbolic representation. For example, if they can physically cut clay or paper pizzas to understand fractions instead of just penciling in paper diagrams or working with equations, they are more likely to grasp the relationship of parts to each other and parts to the whole. In science, students who use the scientific method to actually do an experiment learn more than those who just try to get the right answer by following step-by-step directions to get a predetermined outcome or those who sit back and watch or listen as the teacher explains an activity. When we asked middle and high school students what would make school more interesting for them, the most common response was, "Do more hands-on activities!" Our brains depend on our senses for input. The more senses involved in gathering information, the more data is available for processing.

Young children's ability to develop and use language becomes a powerful tool for using sounds and later written symbols to express thoughts and process information. Although children have already been researching through experimentation, they now move to a deeper level through inquiry by asking lots of questions. The world of learning accelerates until they start school. Regrettably, one of the first things children learn in kindergarten is that teachers ask the questions. Learning seems to do an about-face as children realize they now have to come up with a right answer rather than continue questioning. If they don't know the answer, they begin to wonder if something is wrong with them, especially when others seem to know what to say. Unless given the opportunity to continue researching through inquiry, children slip into a passive recipient mode of school participation. To keep learning alive, we need to make sure we keep students' brains engaged in the process.

> ... the more you learn, the easier it is to learn more.

Brains Are Wired for Learning

Brain research continues to provide amazing insights into the functions and capabilities of the brain. At only 1.4 kg (2 percent of body weight), the brain is a powerhouse of energy consuming an average of 20 percent of the body's oxygen and glucose. Analysis of functional magnetic resonance imaging (fMRI) research reveals increased metabolic activity in the area of the brain responsible for a given task. This activity increases with the difficulty and complexity of a task. We need to understand how to engage students in the kinds of mental activities that stimulate neurochemical reactions in the brain and increase learning capacity. Recent studies indicate that learning and memory directly influence the development and activity of dendrites (Fortin, Srivastava, & Soderling, 2011). Cognitive research explores how the mind uses the brain to take in sensory data, transform them into neurochemical energy, process them for meaning, and build a database for recall, application, and continued learning. Put simply, *the more you learn, the easier it is to learn more.*

To effectively process information, the mind must be reflectively aware of the sensory data or information to be processed. As obvious as this seems, a lack of this ability is one of the key indicators of attention deficits. The senses are the only windows the mind has to the outside world. Once information is gathered for input, the mind transforms the data into mental representations, creating an internal reality through visualization. In this context, visualization includes mental versions of smell, taste, sound, touch, and sight as well as mental representations of symbol systems like language, quantification (numbers and operations), graphics, movements, and music. The mind uses cognitive structures to process available data and make sense of them.

Cognitive structures, which are basic mental tools, process data for meaning by making connections with prior knowledge and experience, finding patterns and relationships, identifying predictable rules, and pulling out wide-ranging principles that transfer and apply to multiple situations. Using effective cognitive structures to process information develops *metability*, a term coined by Garner (2007), which is an interactive dynamic of learning, creating, and changing. Developing metability becomes a major goal of education because it embodies the students' ability to continue improving as a creative learner in a changing world. Cognitive structures can be organized into three categories. For more information on these, see *Getting to "Got It!": Helping Struggling Students Learn How to Learn* by Garner.

1. *Comparative structures*, which include recognition, memorization, conservation of constancy, classification, metaphorical thinking, and temporal and spatial orientation, process information for meaning by comparing how bits of data are alike and different. Teachers often assume students come with this ability. Sometimes, the lack of these mental tools is the missing link that causes that all too familiar blank look, which tells us they don't understand. It's hard for many teachers to imagine what it is like for a student to be sitting in class and nothing makes sense. Without these basic structures, students often drop out mentally early in their educational experience and just drift through years of schooling.

2. *Symbolic structures*, which include language, quantification (mathematics), music, graphics, and kinesthetics, transform data into symbolic representations, so the mind can manipulate and communicate information within a cultural context. Most of the educational process deals with developing and using these structures. However, the comparative structures are prerequisites for these to develop and function effectively.

3. *Abstract logical reasoning structures* include inductive and deductive thinking; analogical and hypothetical thinking; analysis, synthesis, and evaluation; cause–effect relationships; use of propositional logic; and the generation of new information. Helping students develop higher levels of abstract reasoning is both rewarding and challenging because it equips students to become their own teachers. By using Socratic-type questioning and thought-provoking projects and assignments, teachers can stimulate this kind of thinking even with early elementary students.

Since information is doubling at a rapid rate, we are constantly exposing students to new information, often on an hourly basis. We also need to make sure we help them develop the mental capabilities to effectively process massive amounts of information, so it is useful and can be transferred to real-life situations, not just memorized for tests.

Address Relevance and Rigor for Problem Solving

When students ask, "Why do I need to know this?" they are asking a very legitimate question. We have to seriously consider which concepts, skills, and applications are critical in preparing them for life. Notice, this is more than just preparing them for scoring well on a test, for getting ready for the next grade level, or for getting a job. One of our favorite activities in any content area is to give students a problem to solve and then to ask them four questions:

1. How did you figure out what to do?

2. Why did you do it this way?

3. How do you know if this is the best possible solution?

4. How is doing this like life?

The first three questions address systematic reflection to develop rigor, so students are accountable for justifying their own rationale rather than just coming to us and asking, "Is this the right answer?" At first the last question puzzles them, and they don't know what we expect for a response. Gradually, they learn to trust themselves and identify the relevance of the activity as it applies to their own lives.

It takes courage to focus on what matters rather than trying to cover every detail in the curriculum. Muriel, a seventh-grade social studies teacher, started analyzing the content as she prepared a unit on European history and realized with the constraints of class schedules that she had to cover one hundred years an hour to get through the whole curriculum. Fedya, a ninth-grade math teacher, admitted that his curriculum required him to introduce a new concept every other class. He knew his students could not master the information, but kept moving because of the mandated pacing policy in his district. We need to seriously evaluate what we are teaching and how we are teaching it.

Most subjects are taught as discreet separate topics. We encourage teachers to collaborate and integrate studies across the curriculum. Some teams of teachers do this by coordinating topics and activities, for example, studying science, history, and literature related to the same time period being studied in art and music. Another way is using mathematical computations, scientific experiments, and reading and writing activities related to issues in social studies.

With the availability of technology, our challenge is to use it effectively to make teaching and learning relevant and rigorous. Because most students are much more tech-savvy than many teachers, they are valuable assets in setting up ways to make information relevant. We need to be asking what we need to do differently to keep up with the times and develop learning classrooms that prepare students for competency and success in the 21st century. Jacobs (2010) summarized the expertise and wisdom of a team of educational innovators to help us focus on areas that need to be changed. They identified these key areas:

Content: What are the big ideas, the most essential concepts and skills needed for a solid foundation? This includes identifying what to keep, what to cut out, and what to create.

Assessment: What are effective ways beyond testing to demonstrate understanding? These include things like portfolios, simulations, multimedia presentations, performance, reports, generating questions, projects, etc., that are designed, implemented, and evaluated by students.

Organizational structures: What are ways to improve use of time, space, and personnel? This includes divergent ways of grouping students (other than age and grade); grouping professionals for collaboration; accessing community resources; and reconsidering hierarchical administrative practices.

Technology: How do we access and integrate constantly changing techtools to enhance teaching and learning? This includes the need for ongoing professional development, updated equipment and software, continuing support, and reliable security.

Media literacy: How do we inform students, parents, teachers, administrators, and support staff about effective use of media? This includes social media, texting, blogs, YouTube sharing, video streaming, webinars, wikis, podcasts, video productions, hyperlinks, Skype, and the multitude of other platforms available for communication.

Globalization: How are we involving students in issues from a global perspective? This includes the interactive dimensions of every system that affects their lives in regard to issues like economics, food distribution, air quality, security, transportation, health care, politics, and so forth.

Sustainability: What are the long-term effects of innovations in every aspect of life? This includes enduring values and beliefs that impact culture, human wellness, and global interdependence.

Thinking habits: How are we training students and ourselves to effectively process, evaluate, and use enormous amounts of information currently available? This includes developing cognitive structures and habits of mind to systematically make sense of our rapidly changing world.

All of these areas demand rigorous mental and physical stamina for us and for our students to deal with today's problems. We are challenged to reenvision the whole teaching and learning experience.

KNOWING YOUR STUFF AND HOW TO TEACH IT

As professional learners, teachers must have a broad and deep knowledge base, as well as competency in related skills. For example, mathematics teachers, even at the elementary level, have to be proficient in math if they are to effectively teach math. If teachers have a personal aversion for a particular subject, students will pick up a negative undertone associated with that subject without realizing why they don't like it. Megan said, "I just prepare each lesson as it comes and try to stick to the manual in what I say and do, because I was never good at math." Instead of taking the stance of a learner, Megan tried to pretend she was an expert, but her body language and the way she superficially covered the content sent another message. Even though her students might be able to do the algorithms and get correct answers, they will lack a deep understanding of mathematics, which limits their ability to transfer and apply what they are taught.

Elementary teachers are challenged because they usually teach every subject, even though they may have limited competency in some areas. It is acceptable to ask for help, to participate in ongoing professional development in an area of need, and to begin researching more about a particular content. Middle and high school teachers who usually focus on one or two subjects often complain about students' lack of basic knowledge in their content area (frequently blaming elementary teachers for the deficit). This clearly demonstrates that what is taught and what is learned are two different things.

Sometimes teachers are assigned to teach subjects outside their specialties and feel uncomfortable introducing a new concept with which they have limited expertise. Or they might be afraid a student will ask a question they don't know the answer to. The rule of thumb is always be honest if you don't know and welcome the opportunity to model learning together. Anja was always excited when her students came up with challenging questions. Her typical response was, "What a great question! What can we do to find out more about this?"

In one of our professional learning community groups, this situation came up for discussion. Lisa, an experienced teacher, shared what she learned from her grandfather that helped her relax. She said, "No matter how much you know, there will always be somebody who knows more and somebody who knows less." Rob, who was beginning his doctoral studies added, "I found that the more I learn, the more I realize I don't know. It sure keeps me humble!" When teachers are actively learning something new, like a foreign language, they are more aware of what their students are experiencing. It is easy to forget that we are constantly presenting unfamiliar information to our students and expecting them to fully process and remember what we teach. Because of the compartmentalized nature of curriculum, students often perceive lessons as disconnected packages to be memorized. We can help students integrate learning by minimizing artificial boundaries that isolate fields of study. To do this, we need to continually develop expertise in the art and science of teaching and learning.

A Few Fundamentals

Experienced teachers are well aware of the fundamentals of good teaching; however, it is helpful to reflectively review some of the basics and to think about how teachers can help each other continue to improve. It is not enough to just go through the motions when implementing instructions. Marzano (2012) cautions, "I have found that how a teacher uses a strategy is key to how effective the strategy is" (p. 88).

Know Essential Parts of an Effective Lesson

The following are essential parts of an effective lesson:

- Goals and objectives
- Relevant, substantive information (content)
- Effective communication—clear explanations, listening, multi-modal sharing including technology, modeling, and questioning
- Student engagement through questioning, self-directed research, application, hands-on experiences, extended practice for mastery, experimentation, use of technology for research
- Assessment—ongoing for feedback to clarify misconceptions and redirect as needed, formal and informal to assess achievement of

goals, demonstration of understanding through project application and transfer

- Reflective analysis of effectiveness of the lesson

Select Methods and Strategies for Implementation

The array of choices in methods and resources can be overwhelming. We encourage teachers to become familiar with many options and select elements of each that work best in a particular situation. Here are a few we recommend for further exploration because they are flexible, practical, and easily adapted to any age level and content area. These also encourage collaboration, stimulate cognitive development, and give teachers the opportunity to differentiate instruction and assessment.

Flexible Lesson Design (Appendix D). This is a flexible template that can be used for every grade level and subject area. When using this approach, teachers identify the lesson's learning goals and objectives and invite students to explore artifacts, pictures, materials, or other sensory props related to the goal before giving any introduction or explanations. By asking students what they notice and what they wonder about, teachers invite students to bring something to the learning event, to gather sensory data, to make connections with prior knowledge and experience, to activate their natural curiosity and inquisitiveness, and to share their vocabulary related to the concepts to be presented. When using this approach, teachers validate students' input and build on it to introduce the new concepts. Students are then given the opportunity to research, practice, apply, and transfer the information in a variety of ways, so they can demonstrate evidence of their understanding. The last step is reflective evaluation on several levels: What did we learn from the information? What did we learn from the process of participating in the lesson? How can we improve the process to make learning more meaningful? What do we need to learn based on what we now understand? What questions come to mind for further research?

This Flexible Lesson Design is based on action research, sometimes called reflective research, which is discussed in the next chapter. This design provides a practical tool for students to invest in their own learning by making it relevant to their lives. It gives teachers the opportunity to learn with and from their students as they create meaning.

Questioning. Open-ended, higher-order, and Socratic questioning involves more than asking for answers. It takes practice and a change of mindset to become proficient at questioning. Open-ended questions cannot be answered with a simple yes/no or short response. There is no one right answer. Open questions stimulate cognitive engagement rather than recall because students need to process information for meaning and integrate it with prior knowledge and experience. Higher-order thinking questions are based on taxonomies that identify some lower cognitive skills such as recall of facts, comprehending or understanding information, and application as less demanding than higher cognitive skills such as analysis and problem solving, evaluation and synthesis, and creation of new knowledge. These are also open-ended and often used in conjunction with Socratic questioning. Socratic questioning is a way of framing questions to delve more deeply into clarifying and understanding an issue. This powerful approach stimulates cognitive engagement and activates students' ability to answer their own questions. Once teachers are comfortable with this approach, they can use it with students of all ages to help them clarify their thinking, consider information from different perspectives, examine assumptions and biases, and consider implications and consequences of a train of thought. (See Appendix C for examples of Socratic questions.) Although we usually focus on the kinds of questions teachers ask, the real benchmark of our effectiveness as a teacher is *the kind of questions the students ask* the teacher and ask each other.

Workshop Models. Writing workshop, reading workshop, and math workshop models use an interactive organized structure to equip students to take responsibility for their own learning. Elements include the following:

- Guided instruction with both large and small heterogeneous groups to introduce new concepts
- Individual conferencing, centers with computers, texts, and manipulatives for problem solving, practice, and application of skills
- Peer interactions such as pair and share, peer review, and practice for transfer are essential to encourage ownership of learning
- Self-assessment along with formal and informal assessment document achievement of learning objectives
- Science labs, especially those that truly use the scientific method of inquiry, that give students the opportunity to do hands-on research, data collection, and analysis, with real-world implications
- Variations of this approach in the arts and sports, with the availability of multiple resources, where students learn skills and immediately apply and practice to provide evidence of learning

Project Learning. This approach is generally long-term and integrates learning across content areas; involves real-life problems or significant issues, which creates a need for competency in related knowledge and skills; uses inquiry, critical thinking, research skills, collaboration, technology, and multiple forms of communication; and gives students choices in identifying learning goals, methods to achieve goals, and ways to assess and demonstrate effectiveness of the project. This approach also uses experiential, hands-on tasks and is very similar to the action research model. Duckworth (2005) describes this as "critical exploration." She explains,

As a research method, [project learning] has two aspects: 1) developing a good project for the child to work on; and 2) succeeding in inviting the child to talk about her ideas: putting her at ease, being receptive to all answers; being neutral to the substance of the answer while being encouraging about the fact that the child is thinking and talking; getting the child to keep thinking about the problem, beyond the first thought that comes to her; getting her to take her thinking seriously. (p. 259)

The more students do the project planning, organizing, implementing, and evaluating, the more they learn. Trish, a fifth-grade teacher, used one afternoon a week for research. She gave her students a list of topics to choose from. Students didn't know that Trish had created the list based on the state standards for social studies. Students could work individually, in pairs, or in groups. They had to design a project and present a proposal for approval before starting the work. The proposal had to include clearly stated goals and timeline, a rationale for why they wanted to pursue this, what resources and methods they would use to collect information, how they would demonstrate or present their findings, what practical applications their research had for their own lives, and how they would grade or evaluate their work. Their presentation of findings could be oral, written, digital, dramatic, graphic, or any other form they selected. When Trish came to the teachers' team meeting, she shared, "Sometimes I feel guilty that I am not up there doing my 'teacher thing,' but the kids are so excited and so involved, I'm going to use this approach with other subjects."

Personalizing Learning. Students who qualify for special education services are required to have an individualized educational plan to meet their specific needs. We contend that every student should have a personalized educational plan (see Appendix E). At first, this appears to be impossible with large classes at the elementary level and many different classes at the middle and high school levels. When we acknowledge that each student is a unique combination of different capabilities, interests, personality traits, skills, knowledge levels, efforts, needs, styles of learning, motivation, and goals, we must honor diversity and accept it as reality. Too often, we waste time wishing the students were all on grade level and could do the same thing at the same time. It takes creativity, courage, trust, and know-how to recognize and nurture students' ability to take responsibility for their own learning, but we also have to give them the opportunity. Here are some examples of how teachers personalized learning.

Kayo, a third-grade teacher, started each day by writing all of the lesson assignments for the day on the board. Students were allowed to select which assignment they wanted to work on first, second, third, and so on. Each student worked at his or her own pace. Unfinished work was taken home to complete. Kayo spent his time working with individuals or small groups who needed help or teaching mini lessons on new concepts. At the end of April, he shared with his team that he had a new problem. His students had finished the curriculum, and he wanted suggestions on other ideas to challenge them.

Sergio, an eighth-grade math teacher, did a preassessment of his students and decided they were so varied in their knowledge and skills that teaching the group as a whole would bore those who already understood the concepts and totally confuse those who were missing the basics. He set up a portfolio for each student and assigned individual chapters from the text based on their abilities. Students could take the chapter test when they thought they were ready. They had to pass with at least an 85 percent before they could go on to the next chapter. At the end of each chapter, students had to write for their portfolio a reflective analysis of their thinking, why they needed to know this content, and how it applied to real-life examples. Sergio spent his time teaching small groups and coaching individuals who needed extra help. Because students were working with content they understood, they experienced success and gradually built a firm foundation for mathematical understanding.

The more strategies we have in our repertoire, the more flexible we can be in meeting the needs of individual students. The first thing to change is our mindset about teaching whole group the same concepts at the same time.

Identify and Access Available Resources

Although many resources are available through the school districts, consider what the students and their families, as well as the community, have to offer to enrich learning experiences. This is especially true within the multicultural context of our classrooms and the global implications of all learning. Districts usually offer learning coaches, professional development, technical assistance, and other support services as resources. Local colleges, universities, and community organizations can provide other valuable resources in terms of expertise, tutors, and learning experiences of teachers and for students. Chayton was a counselor at an inner-city school where 70 percent of the students were immigrants or first generation American. He worked with a major university in the area to recruit students from many different countries who needed to invest community service hours. These volunteers acted as interpreters in various classes, translated notes to be sent to parents, went with families to meetings with officials, and adopted families to help them adjust to their new surroundings.

With access to the Internet, students can pursue interests and opportunities to enhance their research and pursue significant projects that are relevant to their lives. Online learning opportunities remove some of the long-established limitations imposed by conventional schooling. In a regular classroom, digital resources can supplement or enrich teaching learning interactions. In virtual classrooms, e-learning technology is the primary media for instruction and learning. This format is becoming much more practical in serving students who are unable to attend regular classes or want to do accelerated learning. It is especially suited for students who are independent learners and want to advance at their own pace. The Alberta's Teachers' Association (2011) envisions technology as a tool to enhance learning by giving students more control over their learning, providing more connectivity with parents, giving administrators and teachers proficiency in tracking student progress, and individualizing learning opportunities.

Grant writing is another way to access resources. With a little training, novice and veteran teachers can learn the tips and tricks for preparing successful proposals. It is very exciting to actually have a special budget for projects, equipment, materials, experiences, supplies, training, and other innovations that enrich our teaching and our students' learning. We encourage teachers to go online and identify sources of funding that meet their needs and then to take the risk of submitting a proposal. Many grants are competitive, so it is important to carefully follow guidelines and clearly articulate goals, purpose, implementation strategies, budget, timeline, personnel, and evaluation methods. It is wise to start with smaller grants to develop grant-writing skills; then, involve more colleagues and students with larger grants.

Enjoy the Journey

We believe learning should be fun. It is possible for learning to be rigorous and enjoyable. So, we encourage teachers to keep a sense of humor and be willing to laugh with students while going with them on a journey of competence. Sometimes we concentrate so much on the serious business of teaching that we overlook the powerful advantage of including humor in our lessons. We enjoy taking "brain-breaks" and inviting students to bring clean jokes to share with classmates. When we creatively use humor and novelty with a variety of approaches and activities, we stimulate student engagement, relieve stress, and focus attention. Appropriate use of humor makes content come alive and enhances retention. This is especially beneficial when we encourage students to find funny ways to represent complex concepts by drawing cartoons, illustrating exaggerated characteristics, making a top ten list with comical associations, and using puns or word plays. Body language, facial expressions, changes in voice tone to emulate an animal or cartoon character, gestures, and movements can add emphasis and humor in a way to perk up even dull content. These kinds of techniques help students remember main ideas relevant to the content. Metaphors and analogies are also tools to make connections humorous and memorable. Laughing together helps build student–teacher relationships—students see the teacher as more human and willing to have fun. It also creates a positive, playful classroom atmosphere and demonstrates that learning really is enjoyable for both the students and for the teacher. In all cases, our humor needs to reflect good taste and avoid any kind of hurtful slurs or put-downs. Using humor when dealing with difficult subject matter or before tests helps students relax and think more clearly. We try to pay close attention to the students' level of tension or anxiety and diffuse it by interjecting a funny story or anecdote. Sometimes games are more effective at reinforcing skills than drill and practice. Games that help develop logical thinking, planning, and other cognitive skills are valuable resources that enhance learning on several levels. Invite students to create their own original games related to the content. Enjoy the journey together!

CLOSING THOUGHTS

Although we are required to teach specific content and may even be directed to use specific methods, we design and implement lessons based on our fundamental beliefs about our role and the teaching and learning interaction between teacher and student. We need to understand how students create meaning and how to help them develop the cognitive tools they need to become self-directed, life-long learners. Effective teachers are competent in their knowledge and skills and in their ability to facilitate learning that is relevant, purposeful, and continuous. They use a variety of methods and resources to enhance student engagement. They also surround themselves with mentors and trusted colleagues, so they can continue to grow professionally. The following is a brief summary of some of Eleanor Duckworth's (2006) key points of effective teaching:

- Find ways to present subject matter, so learners create their own thoughts.
- Stimulate students' thinking and their ability to talk about their thoughts.
- Use clear, open-ended questions beyond yes/no responses.
- Provide opportunities for exploration and discussion about projects.
- Listen carefully to students to understand how they process information.
- Evaluate how students see a problem to guide appropriate next steps.

Chart 5.1 compares teaching in a learning classroom with teaching in a managed classroom.

Chart 5.1   Teaching Students in a Learning Classroom vs. Teaching in a Managed Classroom

Teaching in a Learning Classroom	*Teaching in a Managed Classroom*
Define and implement belief about teacher's role as a coach/facilitator.	Define and implement belief about teacher's role as a source of information and skills.
Equip learners to effectively process information for meaning to make it their own.	Require learners to internalize and remember what is presented to score well on tests.
Invest in deeper levels of competency through continuous professional development.	Demonstrate competency in content area, comfortable with level of expertise.
Invite students to bring something to learning situation, and make their connections with prior knowledge and experience.	Expect students to listen, follow directions, and complete assignments.
Engage students in higher level thinking through Socratic questioning, project learning, research, and teamwork.	Ask mostly knowledge and comprehension questions with one right answer.
Experiment with wide variety of methods and resources to enhance learning.	Use limited variety of methods and resources to keep students under control.

REFLECTIONS

After reading this chapter, take a few minutes to reflect on the following:

- How free do you feel to decide what you are going to teach and how you are going to teach it? What is the basis of your decisions? Write a brief reflection on this.
- What is the difference between teaching as transmission and teaching as facilitating? Give evidence in your own practice of each by documenting specific incidents.
- How do you use your creativity to adapt to the learning needs of individual students?
- Compare and contrast how children learn before they come to school and as they go through the schooling system. What recommendations would you offer to stimulate their natural curiosity, creativity, and inquiry?

- What goes through your mind as you plan and design a lesson? How do you identify and select the goals and objectives, activities, and assessments that you use? How do you know if the goals and objectives are achieved? Think about your thinking (metacognition).
- What do think you would do if the lesson bombed or if it took an unexpected turn? How would you capitalize on teachable moments and still focus on your goals?
- What indicators or evidence would show you that you are enjoying the journey of learning?

ACTIONS

- Take a minute to envision your idea of a perfect class. What would make that happen?
- Videotape your class and share it with colleagues to identify and analyze the teacher-to-student, student-to-student, and student-to-teacher interactions.
  - What kind of questions did you ask? How many were closed (one right answer or yes/no)? How many were open (many possible answers)? How did students respond to higher-order questioning compared to basic knowledge or comprehension questioning?
  - What kind of questions did the students ask?
  - What do you notice about your body language and facial expressions and that of your students?
  - How clear were your objectives? Did you achieve your objectives? How do you know? Give evidence.
  - What unexpected teachable moments happened? What did you do about it?
  - What kind of assessments, formal and informal, did you use throughout the lesson?
  - How did you adapt instruction to meet individual needs, capabilities, and interests?
- Design a lesson using the Flexible Lesson Design in Appendix D. Analyze the effectiveness. Invite the students to reflect and evaluate the implementation and their own learning.
- Experiment with a variety of methods such as Socratic questioning and the workshop models. Discuss results with colleagues.

6

How Do We Know If Our Students Are Learning?

How to Assess and Motivate Students

"Assessment is not the destination. It is a marker on the journey of learning, establishing where we are and where we need to go."

—Nic Cooper

"Wait! Let me think! Now I get it!" Mark, a third grader who was on the verge of dropping out mentally because of frustrations and bad grades, responded to his teacher's gentle questioning that encouraged him to take a second look and think about what he had written. Mark suddenly discovered that he could figure things out on his own and self-correct his work. He was excited to find out the task was not as hard as he thought. He looked at his teacher and said proudly, "Now I know I'm not stupid. I did this myself!" His teacher was delighted and shared the moment of celebration. This was a major turning point. Instead of correcting Mark or prompting him with cues, his teacher assessed his learning by asking him to explain why he responded the way he did.

Every day, we are constantly dealing with the question, are they learning what I am teaching? We love to see that bright light go on in students' eyes when they "get it." We struggle to find ways to help those who don't seem to understand despite our efforts to clearly explain concepts, to reinforce and practice what we teach. Assessment is an essential tool for developing a learning classroom. How we assess, what we assess, as well as when, where, and why we assess conveys what is important and identifies criteria for success. Therefore, we have to understand the many facets of assessment. These include the implications of assessment on relationships, relevance, and rigor; the science and art of education; the kinds of assessment including standardized and nonstandardized methods; summative and formative techniques; and analysis of student work as a tool for assessing our own teaching. We also need to be aware of the grading systems we use and determine whether they truly assess what is important. Wiggins (2011) reminds us,

> The goal of all schooling is transfer; the goal is not to get good at school and prove through assessment that you learned what was taught. . . . We must determine if the student is ready for *future* challenges in which they must transfer prior learning. We should look at whether the student can draw creatively and effectively on their repertoire when handling a novel challenge, not merely determine whether they learned stuff. (p. 63)

Assessment practices that target continuous learning emphasize growth and a sense of fairness.

Some of the skills we need to assess in addition to academic achievement include peer and self-assessment, collaboration, and higher level thinking skills. We also have to deal with current grading systems and parental expectations on how assessments are communicated.

RELATIONSHIPS, RELEVANCE, AND RIGOR

Assessment impacts relationships because it establishes the teacher's perspective on what is important and gives students a clear indication of their ability to be successful. Students are more likely to trust their teachers and request needed assistance if they know there are opportunities for improvement without embarrassment. Assessment practices that target continuous learning emphasize growth and a sense of fairness. In a trusting relationship, we have the flexibility we need to take into account varied learning styles and individual needs. When we use assessment designed to communicate a high value on learning rather than emphasis on the grade attained, we instill hope and encourage a growth mindset. Assessment becomes a guidepost along a path, rather than a destination.

With appropriate assessment strategies, we accentuate the relevance and importance of what is being assessed. We benefit as much as the students when we consider how respectful, interactive feedback becomes a guide for improving our teaching as well as documenting students' level of understanding. Learning becomes more relevant when students are encouraged to assess their own work and apply their knowledge to their daily lives for continued growth.

The rigor of assessment depends on its kind and purpose. It is a powerful tool for stimulating deeper thinking, encouraging the need to know more, and developing study habits that benefit students for life. As teachers, we need to formulate test questions that require evidence of understanding rather than regurgitation of memorized information. We fully expect professionals like doctors, engineers, architects, teachers, and others to have competency in their content areas before they begin their practice. This usually requires them to pass rigorous testing as evidence of their depth of knowledge and expertise. At every grade level, we need to carefully evaluate the kinds of questions asked to determine if they are appropriately assessing what needs to be learned.

With these characteristics in mind, notice how the following teachers engender fear or create hope with their stated assessment practices. Consider this question: In what ways might these approaches impact the learning environment of the classroom?

On the first day of class, Ms. Winter always let students know what was expected. She posted her policies and made it very clear she tolerated no exception. She prided herself on the fact that 50 percent of her chemistry students failed every semester because she would not lower her standards.

"OK class, here is what I expect of you in order to pass my class. You will come prepared each day with your homework done. It will be graded and will count toward your final grade. You will be given quizzes as I see the need in order to make sure you are staying up with the work. You will also have projects to complete as well as a test at the end of each chapter. Late work will be graded down. You will lose one full grade for each day that work is late. If you fail a test, it is your responsibility to see me to get help in understanding the things you missed. I am not your babysitter, so I will not hunt you down to make sure you get work done. Grades are given in the typical fashion: A = 90–100; B = 80–89; C = 70–79; and D = 60–69. Anything under a D is failing. Are there any questions?"

All the students knew she meant business. Some were confident they would do well because they had learned how to take tests under these conditions. These students often crammed the night before and cared little if they understood the content—they just wanted a good grade. One student said, "I learned years ago to be a 'mind reader' and figure out what the teacher wants. It's got nothing to do with learning." Others felt confident they would fail no matter how hard they tried. They had little regard for grades and didn't really care what the teacher thought.

Ms. Winter's approach to assessment stifles relationships, has little relevance for her students, and the rigor she espouses neglects to take into account the effectiveness of her teaching. We encourage the teachers to ask themselves, what could I do differently to improve the students' depth of understanding and help them be successful? What are the test scores telling me about how I teach to make information meaningful for students?

Ms. Erby approached assessment differently. When she greeted her class on the first day, she also went over the expectations.

"Ok class, let me first say that I believe that you all can learn and will learn in this classroom. I also understand that some of you might excel in some areas and struggle in others. You are expected to work hard at all times. I will coach you when you falter and assess your progress throughout the year. I will not give up on you. Grading is based on a 5-point system. When we have tests and other assignments, you will be given a clear idea of what is expected. If your performance is poor, and you would like to improve on it, you will be given the opportunity to redo the work or have a different way of showing me you understand the material. I expect you to help each other, work hard, turn things in on time, and be responsible for your own learning. Assessments will include ongoing assignments and final tests as well as your ability to solve problems and apply what you are learning. What questions do you have?"

The students in Ms. Erby's class relaxed. It was clear she was committed to helping them learn. The manner in which she presented her expectations was clear and assured even to those who struggled in other classes that they had a chance to be successful.

These two scenarios demonstrate how assessment affects development of a learning classroom. Using assessment *for* learning instead of assessment *of* learning develops a better learning classroom where students feel hope and are motivated to strive for success.

SCIENCE AND ART OF ASSESSMENT

Assessment is both a science and an art. The science involves objectivity, precision, accuracy of measurement, validity, and reliability based on the kind and purpose of the assessment. Einstein cautioned, "Not everything that counts can be counted, and not everything that can be counted counts." When measuring what is learned, we can only pretend to be objective, because we are constantly using our own or someone else's values to identify what is important. Precision requires an exactness that is totally dependent on the content and degree of expertise being evaluated. Precision is often used in the context of quality. Accuracy relates to correctness of response compared to predetermined standard or value. In geometry, for example, we want students' work to be accurate and their drawings of figures to be precise. Validity identifies if the test question or task actually assesses what it is intended to assess. Teachers often complain that state or national tests are not assessing what they are teaching. Reliability means that a similar test consistently gets comparable results with the same kind of students.

The art of assessment means skill or mastery in using tools to assess learning. It includes teachers' ability to competently select the most appropriate assessment tool, to proficiently interpret results, to creatively use data to enhance learning and improve teaching—much as the art of cooking or the art of music goes beyond the mechanics of doing something technically correct to generating new ideas and involving genius to deftly transform what is mundane and routine into something exceptionally powerful. Although we rarely think of testing as an art form, we challenge teachers to consider how to use the wide variety of assessments available to identify if students are really learning and to use assessment to facilitate learning. Not all assessment data is quantitative (numeric); it includes qualitative information. As pointed out by Tovani (2011),

> Effective assessors know that the purpose of assessment is to see if the instruction is working and students are learning. . . . Effective assessors are always asking themselves, How will students show me their thinking so I can better plan for their needs tomorrow? (p. 70)

Kinds of Assessments

Standardized assessments or tests are one of the most common assessments extensively used in schools. Their advantage is consistency of what is measured across large numbers of students. They are also generally perceived to be efficient, fair, and based on common standards of "what students should know and be able to do." They are systematically administered to measure levels of achievement compared to state or national norms. Standardized scores identify an individual's level of achievement in comparison to knowledge level expectations or *criterion-referenced* content standards. Standardized scores can also be interpreted to rank individuals or groups based on what is normal for other test takers within similar age and grade groups using *norm-referenced* standards. Most standardized tests contain questions such as multiple-choice, true-false, matching sets, or short answer selections, which are designed for computerized scoring. Essay and more open-ended questions and problem-solving tasks that require explanations are more time-consuming and difficult to score. Even trained scorers using benchmarks and rubrics often have difficulty assessing correctness of these types of test items on a standardized basis.

Like many educators, we believe the current overuse of standardized tests limits the curriculum to "teaching the test" and tends to unfairly assess populations for which the tests are inappropriate, such as those who are not proficient in English, have learning difficulties, or come from populations unrepresented when test norms were set. Standardized tests become "high-stakes" when schools are pressured with possible loss of resources or when teachers are threatened with their job because of poor student performance. Although standardized tests may appear to be rigorous, they do nothing to foster relationships and are generally considered irrelevant by students. Standardized tests can be a valuable tool when used appropriately, especially as a pre- and postassessment at the beginning and end of the year. On a larger scale, disaggregated standardized test scores allow for comparisons across schools, districts, states, and programs.

Second, the goal of comparing students against others or school districts against others misses the need for focused and individualized improvement. It suggests that there is a model that if replicated in every setting will create learning. There *are* principles that if followed and individualized in each setting will improve learning. However, the system of labeling "failing" schools and removing resources does little to identify what needs to be addressed.

With so much riding on students' performance on standardized tests, schools are tempted to engage in practices that make performance on these tests the most important aspect of a child's education. This switches the focus from genuine learning to achieving test scores. It encourages schools to "teach to the test," finding ways to devote time to teaching students how to answer standardized test questions or spending time reviewing information believed to be a part of the test rather than progressing with the current curriculum.

When assessment becomes depersonalized to this degree, it does not facilitate individual growth. It is not assessing *for* learning that is moving students along a continuum of growth. It is labeling them and promoting a fixed mindset where students are defined by their scores as being capable or struggling learners. It does not suggest clearly what needs to happen to move them along the continuum of growth when it comes to thinking skills and collaboration. It just tells us what they know at a given point in time.

Effective formative assessments include an element of expert observations and analysis.

Standardized assessments of personalities, learning styles, cognitive abilities, creative abilities, aptitudes, and social interactions are all available tools teachers can use as needed. Detailed discussion of them is beyond the scope of this book.

Nonstandardized assessments take many different forms within the context of a learning classroom. Teachers use end of chapter or unit tests based on curriculum as a *summative assessment* to identify students' level of understanding. These tests can be teacher made, commercially prepared, computerized, open-book, closed-book, project oriented, or creative problem-based applications of content. These kinds of summative assessments can be as simple as a spelling test or as complex as a multimedia presentation. Many nonstandardized assessments are formative in nature; that is, they are ongoing evaluation of learning as it is developing to provide feedback for students and teachers. To personalize feedback, teachers have to know their students, and students have to know and trust that their teacher will respect their questions and efforts. We emphasize the value of a safe learning environment and a trusting relationship for feedback to be effective.

From our experience, we encourage frequent use of formative assessment because it provides opportunities for

1. Ongoing interactions to clarifying misconceptions;

2. Using interactive, open-ended questioning and immediate feedback;

3. Encouraging students' dialogue with teacher and among peers;

4. Stimulating questions from students about their need to know;

5. Responding to teachable moments by modifying instruction or adapting activities to current need;

6. Building relationships based on trust and openness;

7. Enhancing learning by encouraging risk taking and experimentation;

8. Emphasizing the importance of learning and depth of understanding rather than grades;

9. Planning for future learning based on level of competency;

10. Collaborating between students and teachers to make decisions about learning needs.

Effective formative assessments include an element of expert observations and analysis. We encourage teachers to gain proficiency in noticing early signs of confusion to intervene and prevent learning difficulties to steer students toward success. The kinds of questions the teachers ask determine the kinds of responses they elicit. When working with new teachers and with master level teachers, we encourage them to videotape themselves teaching. Once they get over the initial trauma of watching and hearing themselves and actually start analyzing the dynamics of the teaching-learning process, many are surprised to hear themselves answering their own questions or coaching students to get the response they want to hear. It is very exciting when teachers see themselves change what they are doing, for example, asking higher-order thinking questions and stimulating more cognitive engagement among the students.

Marci, an eighth-grade social studies teacher, changed her formative assessment procedures after seeing herself on video. She started looking for the kinds of questions the students ask her and each other. In fact, she changed her homework assignments from answering the questions at the end of the chapter to assigning students to come with at least two questions they wondered about after reading the chapter. She made it clear that the questions were not "knowledge recall" information that could be located in the chapter; they were to be questions that provoked research, stimulated curiosity, and stretched their need to know. This kind of assignment provided formative assessment of students' level of understanding and their commitment to investing in their own learning. The ongoing discussions were student centered and promoted self-assessment by encouraging students to delve more deeply into their need to know the content and how to apply it to their lives.

Ken, a high school algebra teacher, focused on using questioning for formative assessment. After explaining a concept or procedure and giving students problems to work on, he would walk around helping individual students who were stuck by asking questions like "What part do you know for sure?" This way the students were able to self-diagnose without embarrassment and give the teacher the information he needed to clarify misconceptions or guide further learning. With other students who seemed to understand, he would ask, "How would you explain this in your own words to a middle school student?"

We encourage teachers at the end of a lesson, or the end of a day, to simply ask students to write a brief reflection in response to the following questions: What sense are you making of what you learned today? What did you understand from the lessons? What questions come to mind as you reflect on this information? We caution teachers not to be shocked or disappointed if students write "Nothing" because it is important feedback. We also advise teachers to remind students not to just write what they did, but to write reflections about what it meant to them.

ANALYSIS OF STUDENT WORK

Throughout each lesson, we are constantly assessing, sometimes consciously and sometimes intuitively. We encourage teachers to become more reflectively aware of how and why they evaluate students to determine if they are really learning. While teaching, we generally make judgments based on predetermined standards, whether those officially formulated to guide instruction or those personally created to identify what is acceptable. To analyze means to break a whole into component parts and identify the relationship of the parts to each other and to the whole. For example, we can divide language arts Common Core Standards into discrete skills and knowledge units and compare how student work measures up with each part and overall. This enables us to identify strengths and weaknesses. When we analyze, we tend to focus on mistakes rather than strengths. This is a *deficit reduction* model. A more powerful model is *strength enhancement*, which focuses on what you want repeated. To do this, we literally have to change our thinking and look for what the students are doing right. Like students, we respond more positively to encouragement than to criticism that makes us feel incompetent. This approach is much more motivating, builds relationships, and increases rigor by engaging students in their efforts to achieve excellence.

Another way to assess student work using analysis is to look for *cause–effect relationships*. For example, what misconceptions or lack of basic information and skills are causing repeated mistakes? What lack of experience is preventing contextual meaning? What beliefs about learning, emotional blocks, or cognitive limitation interfere with learning? We also need to assess what we could do differently to cause success, like using more hands-on activities, technology, or audiovisuals. We may need to slow the pace, differentiate the instructions, or provide more novelty to stimulate interest.

Teachers can collaborate on analyzing student work through the use of specific protocols. The Small Schools Project website provides some examples of the protocols that can be used. (See www.smallschoolproject.org for more information.) These are defined processes that direct the analysis of student work in a manner meant to create useful, targeted feedback that will help determine if the work is actually meeting the designed objective. When we interpret data from both quantitative test scores and from qualitative descriptive data, we are looking for patterns and themes to gain insights into the meaning of the data. Some examples of qualitative data include things like observations, surveys, photos, journals, interviews, work samples, and other materials. Assessment also includes recognizing anomalies that may provide significant data about how individuals perceive and process information.

Other kinds of assessment data can include attendance records. When we work with students who are struggling in school, one of the first indicators of change in their behavior and attitude toward learning is their increased attendance. They have to be present to learn what we are teaching. Other indicators are fewer discipline referrals, more participation in class, turning work in on time, quality of completed work, cooperation with peers and authority figures, willingness to ask for help, persistence in persevering on a difficult task, more attention for extended periods, and heightened curiosity.

THE SYSTEM WE HAVE

Although we have available a wide variety of assessment tools, we are currently entrenched in a traditional grading system for reporting achievement. There are some principles about grading that we know but pretend to ignore. First, grades limit learning. If learning is an ongoing process, then why should we establish a system that seemingly says a student who gets an A is done learning while one who gets an F has failed to learn? Second, giving grades is a very inaccurate and obscure way of communicating progress. Without comments or a conference, our grading system communicates little to help students learn. Was a particular grade due to lack of effort? Or was there a behavior issue? Or is the student lacking some fundamental skills that need to be remediated? Finally, grades communicate finality and an identity that limits students. For gifted students, good grades label them as "smart" and can make it difficult for them to admit vulnerability or lack of understanding in future classes. For struggling students, bad grades label them as "slow" or unable to comprehend what is taught.

So, what might be the answer? Teachers need to assess students' progress. Schools need to be accountable for their program and its effectiveness. Students need to know where they are in their intellectual and emotional growth. They need feedback in order to grow further. However, that feedback should motivate, not deflate. Too often grades are the only tool for communicating to the students and their families what is being learned. Again, the problem with grades as being the communication tool is that they suggest finality instead of growth.

EXAMINING WHAT IS IMPORTANT

Consider the reality that information multiplies at an astounding rate, making the world our students enter as adults very different from the world of their formal education. Filling them with information, then, is a small part of the equation when it comes to examining what is important.

There are fundamental skills students must learn. But do these skills happen in isolation in their real life? They do not. They happen in a context that is always changing. We tend to think of these fundamental skills as limited to reading, writing, and arithmetic. However, there are other skills that seem to be much more important in the real changing world they face. These skills include the ability to collaborate, the ability to think deeply, and the ability to understand on a deeper level. How are we developing and assessing these?

COLLABORATION

Collaboration is critical because good ideas and solutions come when people share perspectives, listen to one another, refine their work, and keep questioning as they continue to improve. Collaboration doesn't happen naturally. It requires effort and the teaching of specific skills that will promote it. Students who work collaboratively will have a much better chance of being responsible, productive citizens contributing to societal well-being.

Garmston and Wellman (2009) suggest the following norms as critical to establishing a collaborative culture:

> *Those who collaborate hear each other's voices and make every effort to understand each other.*

1. Pausing to allow time for thought

2. Paraphrasing to ensure deep listening

3. Posing questions to reveal and extend thinking

4. Placing ideas on the table and pulling them off

5. Providing data to clarify meaning and build understanding

6. Paying attention to self and others to monitor our ways of thinking

7. Presuming positive intentions to support a nonjudgmental atmosphere

From the Supporting Toolkit for the Norms of Collaboration (http://www.adaptiveschools.com/aspublications. htm#norms). © The Center for Adaptive Schools. Used with permission.

Teaching these norms as fundamental to the process of learning will create learners who see the value in others' ideas and are able to listen effectively. We need to model these to effectively teach them. We also need to give students feedback on their proficiency in using these norms.

Pausing allows listeners to consider the information being shared, to process it, and to formulate clarifying questions or a paraphrase to ensure understanding. Without pausing, we tend to digress into a conversation where listening is replaced with stating and restating points usually at an increasingly higher volume. Those who collaborate hear each other's voices and make every effort to understand each other. When we respond to students this way, we emphasize the importance of pausing to listen.

In a similar way, when we paraphrase, we assure a speaker that we are listening. It is also a way of assessing level of understanding. Paraphrasing is not parroting. It is reflecting key points back to the speaker usually using fewer words. Effective paraphrasing does not begin with "I hear you saying . . ." It typically begins with "So, you . . . ," keeping the focus on the other person. In this manner, the word *so* becomes a way to insert a pause in the response. We need to model this in the manner in which we respond to students.

When we encourage students to explore ideas, assumptions, and various interpretations of issues, we help them focus on learning and gaining insight. This approach stimulates engaging discussions that often create and extend meaning beyond initial expectations. Posing questions that encourage thinking is critical to understanding each other.

During collaboration, we encourage students to take risks and put ideas on the table without fear of judgment as part of the process. We do this with prompts like "What do you see?" "What do you notice?" "What do you think?" "What do you wonder?" We also model how to take ideas off the table without becoming upset when the ideas steer the discussion in an unproductive or irrelevant direction.

A key to eliminating misunderstanding and establishing good communication is providing data to clarify specific points. We do this by asking questions like "So, what do you mean by . . . ?" and "Is your idea then to . . . ?" Data like this help clarify meaning and build understanding.

Often in groups, there are those who may dominate the discussions. In a similar fashion, others may hide and avoid participating. Effective collaboration involves students noticing their tendencies and learning to either assert themselves or quiet themselves if their involvement in the process is impeding it in some way. As teachers facilitate collaboration, they are constantly assessing how students articulate their ideas and work together.

Presuming positive intentions underlies collaboration and positive communication. When listeners become defensive or assume the one speaking is trying to attack or demean them, it is hard to stay out of the lizard brain that activates survival skills of either fighting, withdrawing (fleeing), or freezing. Assuming the other person is making a point designed to further the discussion and improve the solution becomes critical to being able to listen and reflect.

We recommend involving students in peer assessment of various aspects of good collaboration through the use of checklists. This takes practice. Teachers need to make sure students understand how each skill appears when it is being used effectively by asking questions such as the following: What behaviors indicate effective paraphrasing? What evidence is present when someone is presuming positive intentions? These and other questions can be answered by students and will cause them to reflect and more deeply learn why these behaviors are important. (See www.adaptiveschools.com for more information and inventories to rate the use of these norms.)

ASSESSING HIGHER LEVEL THINKING

Assessing students' thinking processes for making meaning is as important as assessing levels of understanding. Most national and state content standards also have process standards that deal with things like metacognition, problem solving, logical reasoning, analysis of underlying assumptions, and evaluation of judgments. We encourage students to think about their thinking and be reflectively aware of how they take in information, connect it with prior knowledge and experience and process it for meaning, store it for recall, and decide how to apply what they learn in a variety of situations.

Bloom's revised *Taxonomy* (Anderson & Krathwohl, 2000) is a practical guide for assessing levels of thinking and a framework for helping students develop more effective thinking processes. Compared to the original taxonomy, the major difference is changing nouns to action verb forms as identifiers for levels of thinking. For example, the most basic level of knowledge is now called remembering; comprehension is called understanding; application is called applying; analysis is called analyzing; synthesis and evaluation are combined as evaluating; and creating takes synthesis to a new level to include generating ideas and information, inventing, planning, and production of novel perspectives.

To help students develop *remembering,* we ask questions that encourage them to reflect and integrate new information with their existing knowledge base in a way that they can access it when needed. For example, what would help you recall this information in another context? How would you make connections with other things you know to help you remember this? What are the main events (characters, interactions, locations, etc.) in the story? Why did you remember these things more than other things? The information for remembering ability is basically descriptive recall—who, what, when, where, and how.

Understanding is developed when students create meaning by comparing bits of information, classifying and organizing data, reflecting on implications, making inferences, and abstracting principles and themes in relationship to each other. We can help students deepen understanding by asking the following questions: How would you explain what this means in your own words? What are the key elements of this concept? How would you diagram this to show how all the parts fit together? As students respond to these and similar type questions, we can assess their level of understanding.

Applying is the ability to take information from the knowledge level to the functional level. Many students can imitate models that we provide and basically do what we do the way we do it. When using this cognitive skill, students can adapt what they understand to familiar and unfamiliar situations. This ability involves making choices and decisions about what knowledge and skill are appropriate for specific situations. We encourage questions such as the following: How would you write instructions to do a specific activity? How would you use this approach in solving a particular problem? If you changed one of the variables or elements in an experiment, how would that affect the outcome? To assess applying ability, we suggest giving open-ended projects, which require students to select appropriate materials, plan step-by-step directions on how to do it, and design method for assessment of quality.

Analyzing is similar to the abilities we described earlier in connection with examining student work. To help students develop this thinking ability, we need to encourage reflection and investigation to identify component parts of a problem, situation, story, task, statement, and so forth. This means breaking it apart like a dissection to probe into deeper meanings under the surface. Questions for analysis frequently start with *why* or *what*. For example, why did this happen? What is the rationale for this decision? What if . . . ? What would happen if . . . ? What are possible causes? What effects will this have? Assessing analyzing is itself an analysis of the process of metacognition. This kind of assessment opens windows of ongoing investigations and is self-reinforcing. Most analysis involves some form of logical thinking like inductive or deductive reasoning.

Evaluating involves judgment in regard to content and process. This means we assess the outcome of things such as an activity, interaction, lesson, situation, or program, as well as the processes involved in getting the outcomes. For example, we may evaluate how an innovation affects learning and also what we learned from implementing the innovation. In art, critiquing a painting or sculpture involves weighing evidence of rendition of the elements of color, form, texture, shape, line, space, and shading. This is similar to using Common Core Standards as criteria for evaluating quality and effectiveness of learning. Evaluating involves values and beliefs. We can help students develop this ability by asking the following questions: How would you rate the overall quality of this sample compared to another? What are the advantages or disadvantages of doing this project? How do you feel about . . . ? How important is this in relation to your goals? This ability is assessed based on credibility of evidence in relation to criteria. Expertise in evaluating comes with concentrated focus in limited area of experience.

Creating as a cognitive ability involves originating something new. The act of creating is generally associated with an "aha!" or moment of insight frequently related to unusual or unexpected intersection of apparently disjointed ideas or possibilities. Creating goes beyond the ordinary and often involves an intuitive leap outside the box of normalcy. This ability is especially valuable in preparing students to be contributors to new technology, medical breakthroughs, scientific research, and unique systems to deal with social issues, inventions, and innovations. We can stimulate this ability by listening carefully to students who come up with ideas that may appear strange at first. By valuing their imagination, we encourage students to approach problems or issues from different perspectives, to consider multiple possible solutions, to stretch their boundaries and experiment with potential discoveries. We can ask the following questions: What are other possibilities? What if . . . ? What happens when you combine . . . ? What would you do to solve the problem of, for example, poverty, social injustice, pollution, crime, AIDS, or bullying if you had all the resources you needed? How many different ways can you do . . . (specific task)? Since most evidence of creating is outside the norms for assessing it, we need to take it for what it is rather than try to limit its expression by grading or scoring it. By its nature, creating in its initial expressions is rarely logical. However, the other cognitive abilities discussed here are used to take the original ideas and put them into practical application.

SELF-ASSESSMENT AND PEER ASSESSMENT

What can be learned from assessing others? What can be learned from assessing oneself? Imagine the investment students might have in assessing their own and each others' work if they helped identify the criteria for excellence in a project or assignment. It's a great learning experience! When we work with students to establish criteria to assess learning, we need to frequently review why these are important, the kind of evidence needed, and the rating method used. For example, students need to discuss what they would look for in a great presentation, excellent project, or quality work. Students who help establish criteria take more responsibility for their own learning and often evaluate themselves more rigorously than the teacher. When teachers include students' input as a significant part of their summary assessment, students feel valued.

This is particularly powerful in classrooms where the emphasis is on learning and continued growth because students are empowered to help each other. Classrooms that emphasize competition and grades lessen the impact of these types of assessment practices, because students feel pressured to pronounce judgment rather than give feedback.

GRADING METHODS

But what about the grades? In most traditionally managed classrooms, grades are generally based on how students regurgitate information, rather than how well they can use it or give evidence of understanding Most schools are largely confined to a system that mandates grades of A through F based on a 100-point scale. This scale is often seen as sacrosanct and rarely questioned. However, it needs to be questioned on many bases. Why is it scaled to promote failure (for example, 59 percent chance of failing)? What do these grades mean? Are *excellent*, *above average*, *average*, *below average*, and *failing* adequate to assist students in their learning?

We need to ask, do grades motivate students? Yes, if students have felt rewarded for being successful in giving teachers what they want. Usually the answer is no, if students experience failure. When students get an A, there is little impetus to continue learning. When students get an F, they lose hope and motivation to engage in the process. *Grades set limits based on what the teacher knows and wants students to know.*

To motivate learning, we need to examine grading through the lens of adolescent video game players. What keeps them in front of those games so long? Why is it so addictive? Graphics, action, and excitement perhaps are a part of it. But also examine how they are designed. The player succeeds at a level and is given a new, harder challenge, but one that is achievable. The players then attack that level with confidence that they will succeed. Players also are aware of their level and how they are progressing. Encouragement is built into the system as is novelty and challenge. These factors produce a focused motivation, which has been described as flow. According to Csikszentmihalyi (2008), *"flow" happens when the task is challenging but achievable.*

Consider the following descriptors for the levels of attainment—to replace the A through F grades:

1. Struggling to learn—preoccupied; not making connections; unfocused; more individual assessment needed

2. Learning—gaining insight; beginning to understand

3. Emerging—beginning to apply learning

4. Demonstrates mastery occasionally

5. Demonstrates mastery regularly

6. Teaches concepts to others

These labels are tools to more clearly communicate levels of learning with parents and students.

Performance assessments are more effective than grades, because they require students to demonstrate or explain their thinking and give practical examples of how the information applies to situations other than those provided in class. To make grading more useful and to communicate information relevant to the students' learning, we need to consider two important characteristics of assessment. First, learning is more than remembering facts; it involves higher-order thinking skills for making sense of information. Second, proficiency is evident in reference to specific standards. This is much better than an A in algebra, or even more significantly a C, where neither the student nor the parent really understands where a student needs help. *Effective teachers are in the business of creating students who will potentially become smarter than the teacher.* If the goal of assessment is to help us understand how to facilitate learning, then we need to involve those being assessed and use results to guide our instruction.

To communicate the idea of growth along a continuum, we sometimes use graphs to visually represent progress along with using descriptors. When students receive feedback in this manner, they see learning in a manner similar to the way they may see their progress on a video game.

They know where they are and can clearly see the next challenge. This gives them confidence in their ability to succeed and motivates them to continue trying.

But what will the parents think? Although we encourage teachers and administrators to experiment with alternative grading methods, they encounter what appears to be an impenetrable barrier of parental and political expectations. Based on their own schooling experiences, parents and politicians resist any innovations that appear to rob them of their ability to compare their students' success with that of others. They note that colleges rely on grade point averages (GPAs) to evaluate for admission. They also contend that competition supports learning and that winners and losers are a fact of life.

Enlightened educators know differently. The premise that grades are important to compare students is faulty. The goal is learning. Assessments are tools to communicate where students are at a point in time along a continuum of growth. Although colleges now rely on GPAs, this could change if we used a more accurate system for communicating students' thinking ability and skill levels. Competition does not enhance learning. Competition is for athletic events and sales quotas. Even in these situations, outstanding athletes and sales professionals learn from others to improve their performance. Great teams support each other to succeed. In the real world, professionals in medicine, business, law, and other fields learn from others and collaborate to solve problems.

Another problematic aspect of the current grading system is the emphasis on summative assessments. At its most problematic, it includes the overemphasis on standardized tests. Schools also emphasize common assessments at the end of units of study. Teachers lament that they need to use grades or other shorthand methods of sharing progress because of the time constraints. When schools have attempted to eliminate grades and just use comments, the task becomes overwhelmingly time consuming.

CLOSING THOUGHTS

The practice of summarizing achievement at the end of a study focuses on the grade as an end product. It does not lend itself to helping students plan for success by gaining a better understanding of where they are on a continuum of learning. For example, if students receive a C, they know they are average. What does this tell them they need to do to improve? Work harder? But what skills should they target? What do we know about how they think or work with others?

The overemphasis on standardized tests suggests students are products of the learning environment. Put them through a good school, and they come out "smart" at the other end. The idea that students are like widgets and can be judged using standard quality control measures is faulty on a number of levels.

In contrast, if students receive feedback on their ability to think along a continuum applied to targeted objectives, they and their parents know what skills need to be developed for learning and for collaborating with others.

The purpose of education is developing learners who have proficient thinking skills to understand and apply information and who work well with others to solve complex problems and create new knowledge. The process of teaching and learning is a dynamic cooperative interaction, not a one-way transmission of information. Politicians contribute to the success of our educational systems by providing financial and policy support. Parents are critical collaborators who have longitudinal information about their children (knowledge of them over time), while teachers have latitudinal information (knowledge of students at this age). Allowing uninformed people to reform our schools, and in this case our assessment practices, is like a passenger on a bus complaining about a bumpy ride and insisting on thicker seat cushions to improve the problem. The focus is misplaced. A mechanic, the expert in this case, will focus on the shock absorbers and fix the problem more permanently. The seat cushion fix will never fix the mechanical problem leading to the bumpy ride.

We, as professional educators, need to take responsibility for improving schools and working with parents and politicians to help implement changes to develop learning classrooms based on relationships, relevance, and rigor. Chart 6.1 summarizes characteristics of assessment in a learning and a managed classroom.

Chart 6.1   Assessing Students in a Learning Classroom vs. a Managed Classroom

Assessing Students in Learning Classrooms	Assessing Students in Managed Classrooms
Assessment is ongoing and formative with feedback for students and teachers.	Assessment is summative at end of units with grades given by teacher.
Assessment marks growth along a continuum.	Assessment stresses performance at a point in time.
Thinking and collaboration skills are included in the assessment feedback.	Feedback is focused on knowledge retained and reported on tests.
Next learning steps are clearly suggested by assessment feedback.	Only current situation is described; next steps are unclear.
Teachers use assessment data to adjust practices to develop deeper thinking and collaborating skills and enhance learning.	Teachers use assessment data to judge performance of students and decide what they know and need to know next.
Teachers teach parents and public officials about the need for a focus on thinking skills.	Schools respond to the demands of parents and public officials accepting their perspective as being expert.
Multiple modes of assessment are used to track the development of thinking skills.	Formal assessment practices compare groups of students.
Assessment practices motivate growth and create hope for success with all learners.	Assessment practices motivate capable learners while potentially limiting and demoralizing struggling learners.

REFLECTIONS

After reading this chapter, take a few minutes to reflect on the following:

- Think about the manner in which various assessment and or grading practices have impacted your learning. In what ways did they motivate you? In what ways did they limit you?
- Consider how you responded to a poor assessment in some area of your life. What impact did this have on your mindset? Did you grow from it? Did you feel like you failed and decide to give up? What contributed to your response?
- Consider how you responded to a positive assessment. Did you continue to improve and strive to gain more knowledge? What contributed to your response in this situation?
- Reflect on the connections between effective assessment and relationships with students.
- How relevant are your assessments in terms of facilitating learning? How rigorous are you in setting standards of quality that are achievable?

ACTIONS

- Review your assessments of students from the previous year. What do they tell you about your students' ability to think at various levels? Note how you might adjust them to give more information about students' thinking skills.
- Review your grading practices as well as your instructional practices. What are you doing to promote healthy collaboration? What more can you do to make this a focus?
- Record a video of yourself teaching. Analyze interactions, levels of cognitive engagement, and the kinds of questions you and your students ask.
- Meet with some colleagues to discuss how you might redefine your assessment practices to provide better growth-oriented feedback for your students.
- Examine your common assessments to determine their focus. How do they promote deeper thinking? How do they suggest next steps for the learner and the teacher?
- Analyze student work for causes of misconceptions, levels of understanding, and processes involved in problem solving or doing task. What does student work tell you about your teaching?
- Discuss with other teachers how you might collaborate with parents to implement alternative assessments.
- Discuss with parents this perspective and listen to their concerns, noting what you think they need to know while gaining new insight into what they feel they need.

7

How Do We Stay in the Game?

How to Cultivate Learning Communities for Continual Professional Growth

"In times of change, learners inherit the Earth, while the learned find themselves beautifully equipped to deal with a world that no longer exists."

—Eric Hoffer

Developing a learning classroom is an ongoing process of balancing who we are with the person we want to be, who students are with the learners they are capable of becoming, what we know with what we need to know, and what we want to do with what we can do.

Regardless of the circumstances, to achieve balance and sustain growth, we have to stay on top of our game. It is one thing to know a team sport and another to play a winning game where everyone pulls together to implement an effective plan of action. Our challenge is to keep improving the knowledge and skills we need for teaching and learning and to focus with purpose, passion, and persistence on attaining and sustaining relationships, relevance, and rigor.

RELATIONSHIPS

Earlier in the book, we discussed the importance of relationships with students and parents. In a school setting, we also need to develop meaningful relationships with administrators, colleagues, support staff, specialists, school board members, and professional organizations. This includes identifying the various roles everyone plays within the dynamics of the school. It is usually obvious who is in authority, but it takes a certain amount of savvy to discern who has more powerful influence on how things are done. We encourage teachers to resist the temptation to just do their own thing in isolation. Sometimes, this may appear to be the road of less resistance; however, it will surely stifle growth.

To continue growth as the days, weeks, months, and years march on, we need to surround ourselves with support groups of trusted colleagues who will encourage ongoing professional growth, provide honest feedback, share ideas and resources, help with problem solving, and celebrate our successes. New teachers benefit from the coaching of mentors with whom they can frequently conference about day-to-day operations. Experienced teachers benefit from the wisdom of others when they are willing to reflect and learn together in a trusting relationship.

On a personal level, we also need to maintain our relationships with family, friends, neighbors, community, and social groups. *We are not our job.* Teachers who take time to balance their personal and professional lives are more effective in every aspect of their lives. We encourage teachers to take time to relax and have fun, so they can be themselves and develop more meaningful relationships.

RELEVANCE

To keep growing and make sure our teaching and interactions with the students are relevant, we have to keep current on research, technology, and current events. When we develop a certain level of competence, it is easy to slip into a kind of static comfort zone without even realizing it. Participating in seminars, coursework for advanced degrees or certifications, personal action research, in-depth study of interesting topics, staying in tune with the media, and listening to feedback from students are some ways to continue adapting lessons for relevance. With technology, free professional development is available online with webinars, educational blogs, YouTube videos, and discussion boards. Marzano, Frontier, and Livingston (2011) remind us, "Technology can provide powerful opportunities to organize teachers within schools, across the district or state, or nationally or globally to supplement and expand face-to-face professional learning communities" (p. 78).

Our challenge is to focus on what matters and balance the importance of basics with the need for current applications and implications.

Relevance encourages students to bring something to the learning experience and stimulates cognitive engagement.

RIGOR

"By choosing challenging content and creating lessons that require students to think critically, flexibly, and creatively, you can help them exceed course standards and build their capacity and engage in highly rigorous thinking and learning" (Jackson, 2011, p. 24). Rigor is an essential element of sustaining relationships and relevance in ongoing professional development. We need to stay abreast of national, state, and local standards, benchmarks, and requirements if our students are to be successful. We also need to understand them at a broad and deep level, so we can extend our students' learning across subject areas. When implementing these standards in the classroom, rigor also requires personal integrity, fairness, and transparency. To keep focused on the business of learning can be challenging when the pressures of public accountability put everything we do under scrutiny.

In order to accomplish this and maintain our own growth, we need the support of a community of learners within our school where it is safe to develop the trust necessary to examine our work, our students' work, and to seek connections in ways we might not recognize on our own. It requires the integrity to open ourselves to feedback and to keep searching for new ways to ignite thinking with our students.

When asked what they most admired about a teacher, many successful students say things like "He was strict, but fair!" Even though they may seem to resist, students appreciate the security of structure and consistency. This is only possible if we have the self-discipline to make the tough decisions that protect the rights and responsibilities of teachers and learners. Rigor also requires that we live by the same rules and expectations that we make for our students, especially in terms of quality and excellence of work. If we expect students to be punctual or turn their work in on time, we also have to be punctual and give them feedback in a timely manner. If we expect respect, we also have to give respect.

SCHOOL CULTURE

As teachers, we function within a school culture. The term *culture* has hundreds of meanings. In this context, we are looking at school culture based on the definition by the United Nations Educational, Scientific and Cultural Organization (UNESCO): culture is the "set of distinctive spiritual, material, intellectual and emotional features of society or a social group . . . that . . . encompasses, in addition to art and literature, lifestyles, ways of living together, value systems, traditions and beliefs" (UNESCO, 2001). Simply put, culture is the "way we do things around here" (Cunningham & Gresso, 1993, p. 20). Without realizing it, we are so immersed in the status quo of how things are done that it is difficult to imagine how things could be different. Much like the fish in the water, which has never experienced a different environment, we tend to accept schooling for what it is.

We have been in education long enough to see many innovations come and go. We have worked with courageous teachers who dream of starting their own schools where things could be done the way they need to be done. Yet those teachers get caught up in the realities of conforming to traditional approaches. Somehow, the cookie-cutter model of grouping students by age and grade, putting them through a series of predetermined lessons, and testing them with the same standardized tests remain a pervading paradigm. If we are going to influence the culture of school, we first have to become aware of what the spiritual, material, intellectual, and emotional features of our particular school, as well as the value systems, traditions, and beliefs that govern ways of doing things.

Sometimes we can find ourselves engulfed in a negative school culture where fear and cynicism are rampant. Schools are made up of people and as such can respond to systemic stress much as individuals in the schools do. This may involve focus on survival by reacting to economic, social, and political pressures rather than being proactive to prevent problems. Reactive solutions are usually cosmetic and short-term in nature. In these situations, decisions are often made by a few with little input from those who are impacted by the decisions, and sharing with other colleagues is infrequent or nonexistent. In a negative school culture, teachers fault students for lack of ability or unwillingness to learn. Data from standardized tests are used to document progress on a competitive basis rather than to analyze for ways to improve. In an unhealthy school culture, teachers can be easily swallowed up in feelings of insecurity, much as a child in a chronically stressed family. They tend to adopt ways of coping focused first on survival and last on the overall goals of engaging learning. All of this causes stress and inhibits development of a positive learning culture.

It is easy to get trapped trying to be all things to all people, feeling unappreciated, or letting ourselves be intimidated by outspoken persons on staff. Working with individuals who are friendly and cooperative is easy. Learning to get along with those who tend to be negative, cynical, brash, or critical is challenging. The more secure we are in our personal identity, the less threatened we are by others with different opinions or ways of doing things. By consciously setting parameters of what is acceptable, we literally train people how to treat us.

If we find ourselves in a toxic working environment, we need to focus on our own practice without trying to change everyone else. This begins with self-awareness. Much of what was discussed in Chapter 2 becomes even more important in this type of situation. Learning about our own history and understanding how this influences our behavior helps to neutralize negativity and connect positively with our students to learn with them and from them.

To create a positive school culture focused on learning, we need to recruit colleagues and administrators who have the courage to envision change and focus on developing learning classrooms. Teacher leaders who embrace the process of learning as the primary focus in their classrooms can make a difference over time within systems, even toxic ones. These teachers and administrators become the conscience of the school in the sense of maintaining the focus on teaching and learning, no matter what situation arises.

Highly effective school systems communicate vertically to establish a school systemwide culture. These systems establish similar practices at all levels, are consistent in teaching their students to work hard and care for one another, and make

> *Successful schools see obstacles as challenges, not limitations.*

learning the focus throughout the system. This type of vertical alignment (consistency between levels) requires a high degree of collaboration between professionals and a commitment to professional conversations and learning. When this is present, the work is energizing. When it is not, it is more challenging. However, committed teachers can still make a difference.

Eric was sitting in a staff meeting as the principal spoke about upcoming cuts in budget and the fact that it may alter their program. The principal's tone was one of despair. He spoke with sadness and frustration. The staff reflected these feelings, with many openly and angrily criticizing the decisions. Eric listened intently to what was being said before he offered this perspective:

"OK folks, it appears that we have a reality here that is going to challenge us. We are going to be charged with doing more with less, not an uncommon situation actually. So instead of focusing on what we don't have, let's focus on what we do have and how we can create the best program we can with the resources we have?"

Successful schools see obstacles as challenges, not limitations. One courageous principal, leader of a nationally recognized middle school, approached cuts by always finding a way to add something that would benefit everyone. This might be a program, an approach, or some new technology that he funded from an outside source. Teachers who embrace growth will examine and question all premises. They will ignite passion by being the positive voice, which helps everyone grow professionally within the school community. They will embrace community and create it on every level.

COMMUNICATION

Critical to effective growth and working through concerns is the ability to communicate effectively. This includes listening attentively. Teachers in any school environment can help each other grow and facilitate change by working diligently on understanding others' perspectives. Mastering the skill of pausing and paraphrasing is a good way to model this and to build credibility with others. Garmston and Wellman (2009) list these as two critical norms of collaboration for building adaptive schools that fluidly create professional learning communities (PLCs).

Often when we have strong convictions about a subject, we feel compelled to explain to others our perspective very clearly and directly. When they don't agree, the tendency is to be more vigorous in our presentation of our viewpoints. This can get louder and become very frustrating at times. Rarely, however, do others change their minds because we are stating our perspective louder and more forcefully. It is similar to when we encounter someone who doesn't speak our language. Our first response might be to speak louder and slower. It is not the speed or loudness of our speech that is the issue; it is the language. When we keep reasserting our ideas more vigorously, we are ignoring the fact that we do not understand their language, or in this case, their perspective. It is time to listen more effectively.

In contrast, if these conversations began with a sincere desire to first understand the other person's perspective, the situation changes markedly. This requires self-discipline. The first step, pausing, allows us to restrain our impulse to straighten them out and to reflect on what they are saying. This keeps us from reacting and allows us to listen carefully, rationally process what they are saying, and then briefly summarize what they said, so we can actually establish a connection for real communication. Once connected, we can state our thoughts and feelings. The tricky part is that the other person may not be as aware of effective communication, and we may find ourselves listening to a louder assertion of their perspective. If we resist responding in kind, we still have a chance of being heard while learning more of their perspective. By pausing and paraphrasing again, we again model good communication and respect for their views. When this process doesn't progress to true understanding as shown by the other person attempting to summarize our perspective, it is always acceptable to give a prompt. This is how that may look.

Andy sees Pete and decides to share his excitement about a workshop he's just attended on PLCs.

"Hey Pete, how are you?"

"Doing OK, Andy. What's up?"

"Well I just got back from the PLC workshop and it was amazing. I believe it can really make a difference here if the staff can be open to it."

"Yeah, well good luck with that. We've had tons of that 'touchy-feely' stuff over time, and it doesn't ever seem to make any difference. I don't think you'll ever sell that with this staff."

Pete pauses, "So, you think the staff will associate PLC work with previous efforts and won't want to try again."

"Yeah, that's right. It's flavor of the year around here."

"Well, this might be different, Pete. This guy emphasized how we really desire to be a part of a community and that, by working together and teaching the skills it takes to collaborate effectively, it can happen over the long-term. That's something I think we've been missing. We've never really sustained work on skills of collaboration at all, let alone over time."

"Yeah yeah, I know, this is different. You know how many times we've heard that? Nothing's going to change. You really think that they will keep the focus on one thing over time? Not going to happen. Makes too much sense."

"So, you believe that there is too much negativity to ever progress from where we are then."

"I guess that pretty much sums it up. I can tell you this much; it would take a lot to make me invest in another approach."

"I see, so if you really believed it was worthwhile, you might check it out though."

"Maybe."

"Andy, as you listened to what I was saying, what did you hear that might be different?"

Andy thinks for a second and then says, "The part about sustaining work on skills over time and I guess focusing on collaboration instead of a specific new program."

"Great, that's a good summary of what got me excited. I'll let you know more as I learn more also. Thanks for listening, Andy."

Pete resisted arguing with Andy in this scenario. He paraphrased each of Andy's comments, then probed for the opening where Andy might hear him. By asking him to tell him what he might find different, Pete was establishing the "open place" where he could focus his efforts. It is significant that Pete thanked Andy for listening. This plants the seed that listening is valued.

Refraining from gossip, dominating others, or being dominated often means listening for feelings rather than content. Cynics are fearful of change. Attacking a frightened (cynical) person will exacerbate their fears. As discussed previously, listening but not adopting or validating their perspective while paraphrasing the emotions that underlie their negativity may open up some vulnerability. That vulnerability could allow them to be open to another perspective if they acknowledge their feelings. If not, it is out of the teachers' sphere of influence.

Although it is tempting to denigrate and attack those who are cynical, teachers who lead others effectively and embrace growth, presume positive intentions with their colleagues, listen well, and thoughtfully consider divergent views. They are not afraid of conflict but keep the conflict focused on ideas and not on feelings. They are assertive in their views while being able to listen and understand the views of others. Learning communities evolve from those who approach their collegial relationships like this (Garmston & Wellman, 2009).

One of the points that Andy made in the previous scenario was the commonly labeled phenomenon of the "new flavor of the year." Someone goes to a workshop and that becomes the new focus. That focus, however, isn't sustained and is replaced by next year's focus. Over time, this creates *change fatigue,* the result of constant change with no clear, central purpose.

Teachers can impact this process by asserting themselves into the decision-making discussions wherever possible. By assuming leadership positions, and then by being faithful to the central purpose of ongoing and sustained learning, new ideas and programs are filtered to fit with what is in place.

New approaches and programs are not useful when they denigrate or redefine the previous approaches without a clear understanding of how this will be better. Not only are the benefits important; so is the smoothness with which changes can be made and sustained. When abrupt changes are made without honoring the previous efforts and building bridges, those invested in former approaches are discounted and can become resistant. The organizing questions to assess new approaches are the following:

- How will this improve teaching and learning?
- How will we transition from what we've been doing and honor previous efforts?
- How will we sustain growth over time?

With those in place, growth can be focused and purposeful. Becoming skilled in effective communication helps us to build a positive school culture. It helps maintain balance and focus on building a learning community among teachers that becomes a model for learning classrooms. It also stimulates reflection that can lead to more systematic reflective research on issues affecting effective practice.

REFLECTION IN ACTION

Reflecting on an ongoing basis on our teaching, sharing ideas with colleagues, examining student work with other teachers, and engaging in professional reading with others are all ways to take responsibility for our own growth.

Documenting reflections with journal writing makes it possible to identify patterns and systematically improve our practice. Writing a journal is more than narrating what happened. It is questioning and analyzing incidents, comments, thoughts, feelings, interactions, actions, challenges, and possibilities. This process helps improve the depth and breadth of our understanding of teaching and learning. Healthy reflection and sharing in these situations requires honest and reflective feedback designed to clarify issues and to identify situations that require action. It does not help to commiserate or give solutions. It does help to paraphrase and empower to act on solutions that we or colleagues may identify.

Engaging in reflective action research creates energy. To do systematic action research, we first identify a question, concern, or issue directly related to our everyday practice. For example, we might ask, "What happens when I . . .?" Since this approach facilitates change, and *we can only change ourselves,* it is important to keep the focus on what we are doing, rather than trying to change students or anyone else. We encourage teachers to start small with very specific issues and a short timeline to develop reflective research skills. Next we identify what data would help us address the issue and how we will collect the data within a given timeline. Data can be observations, journal entries, photos, videos, interviews, student work, test scores, e-mails, student comments, and other forms of documentation. Once we have some data related to our question or issue, we begin to analyze them, looking for patterns and ways to interpret what the information means. It is very helpful to take the data and our preliminary analysis to a group of trusted colleagues for further analysis and feedback. Based on what we learned from the data and analysis, we design a plan of action to outline what we could do differently to improve or answer our question. As the plan is being implemented, we evaluate its effectiveness and also reflect on what we have learned from doing the research. This process is cyclical and inevitably leads to more questions, usually on a deeper level. In this way, reflective research becomes a powerful tool for self-directed, ongoing professional development.

As active researchers, teachers model learning based on inquiry and simultaneously stimulate students' natural learning capabilities. We encourage teachers to use a simplified procedure to engage in ongoing mini research projects that help them focus on improving their own practice by systematically collecting and analyzing data in collaboration with colleagues.

1. *Identify a question* or issue to be studied: What do you want to know?

2. *Collect data* about the issue through observations, interviews, records, reports, student work, or journals: How will you find out information about what you want to know?

3. *Collaborate with colleagues to analyze the data*: What did you learn from the data you collected and analyzed?

4. *Develop and implement a plan of action*: What are you going to do differently based on what you learned from the data?

5. *Evaluate implementation of the plan*, write a brief summary, and formulate new questions: What did you learn from doing this research?

Teachers who have participated in this kind of self-directed, ongoing learning have discovered new purpose and energy in their work.

Susan, an elementary teacher, stated, "I finally found a way to get answers to my puzzling questions, but I was surprised to find that doing this research just kept bringing up more questions." Emil, a middle school teacher, said he thought he was doing a good job before he started this kind of research, but when he watched videotapes of his teaching and showed them to his students, they helped him see how he could do things differently to facilitate learning.

Many teachers reported that using this approach helped them focus on the real meaning of teaching and learning. Mini-teacher research is a tool that equips us to systematically examine our practice and benefit from our own learning experiences. This kind of active learning exemplifies ongoing professional development because it is directly related to our current job and can be easily integrated into our daily schedule. It is systematic and results oriented. It is collaborative and encourages open, honest dialogue that stimulates ongoing questioning and self-evaluation in recursive cycles of research.

As teachers become comfortable with this approach, they find it is exciting to invite students to follow a similar model and use available technology to reactivate their natural curiosity, creativity, and inquisitiveness. The Flexible Lesson Design (Appendix D) provides a practical way to design a lesson that follows the action research model.

Reflective research is a very positive way to do professional development while facilitating learning. Engaging in action research and sharing results can help move a static system to one that is dynamic. One way to engage in this type of research is to consistently reflect on teaching on a day-to-day basis. Teachers who examine and note how a lesson progressed,

---

1. What do I want to know? Identify question, concern, or issue.

2. How will I find out? Collect relevant data.

3. What sense do I make of the data? Analyze and interpret data.

4. What will I do about it? Make a plan of action and implement it.

5. What happened and what did I learn? Evaluate plan, reflect, and identify a new question.

recognizing what worked and what didn't, are more likely to grow from their experiences. These reflections should include an analysis of the students, the circumstances of the lesson on that day, and any other factors that may have either enhanced or diminished the lesson's effectiveness. Another way is to do case studies of individual students and their work to see how to help them more effectively. Making this practice routine keeps the work exciting and opens doors to new approaches.

Teachers embracing ongoing growth will also challenge new approaches with insightful questions grounded in research. They are not susceptible to pop trends, keeping their attention on what will last and what is consistent with what has been successful. Sustaining growth over time by improving approaches rather than discarding them and trying every new trend is a powerful way to create and maintain momentum. It enhances a feeling of purpose. It also enhances the feeling of efficacy among teachers, gives them a voice, develops leadership, and empowers them to make a contribution to the profession.

BUILDING ON STRENGTHS

Too often, we tend to focus on our weakness or things we do wrong. It is much more effective to focus on our strengths. As we do more of what we do well, we are more likely to get better in so many ways that we are better able to be honest about how to improve. The same thing happens when we take the time to encourage and compliment our colleagues. In many schools, recognition of a job well done is rare. We can, however, make this a part of promoting growth for each other in a climate that encourages commitment to purpose, evidence of passion, and dedicated persistence to ensure success for all.

> *Passion requires that we examine and embrace our successes, while examining and embracing failures as just the next step to success.*

Purpose

We encourage teachers to write their purpose in life—personal and professional—and to keep it constantly available for review. This is not the same as a carefully crafted mission statement that hangs on the wall of the school and has little or no impact on daily practice. Reflection on our purpose keeps our focus on our goals and simplifies our lives by guiding our thoughts, decisions, words, actions, feelings, and plans. Everything is aligned to support and enhance what really matters. This protects us from becoming overextended or distracted. We stay in tune with that inner voice that keeps us aligned and peaceful. No matter what may happen on the outside, our professional purpose asks, how will this enhance learning? With that as the central focus, reflective journaling and conversations can help to keep us focused.

Passion

A key ingredient of passion is unrelenting energy, commitment, and excitement. Passion requires that we examine and embrace our successes, while examining and embracing failures as just the next step to success. Focusing on gratitude when circumstances seem overwhelming can help avoid hopelessness or a feeling of helplessness.

Sustaining passion requires both internal and external support. Internal support involves keeping ourselves healthy—physically, emotionally, and spiritually. External support involves collaboration with others who are like-minded and with whom we can share our concerns and receive support. These groups of people can be sources of energy when ours wanes. They can also provide sounding boards when we feel we need to clarify our thoughts and feelings. In any case, passion sustains our ability to negotiate the stresses of our profession.

Persistence

The idea of never giving up on our mission, our students, or ourselves is a critical aspect of successful teachers. These teachers expect miracles. Often just by their persistence, miracles happen. Students who may have given up see someone supporting them, challenging them, and expecting great things from them, and they make a decision to change. Being persistent requires allying with those with a similar view of the world while becoming emotionally impervious to the temptations of cynicism.

A FINAL WORD

The goal in writing this book is to provide a basis for teachers to use as a way of developing classrooms that promote learning. Learning doesn't happen without reflection, so the inclusion of reflective questions at the end of each chapter is consistent with this purpose. For classrooms to be safe, engaging places in which students learn at their highest level, teachers need to know themselves, know their students, grow in their teaching ability, collaborate with others to build community, and be resourceful. "Among synonyms for resourcefulness are imagination, perseverance, artfulness, canniness, cleverness, deftness, facility, and inventiveness. How cool to perceive one's job as honing those attributes!" (Tomlinson, 2012). Embracing challenges, staying positive, believing in miracles, and being at peace with oneself are all critical to helping teachers to stay in the game and enjoy the journey.

As we thought about the importance of relationships, relevance, and rigor, we recalled the interaction we observed between an experienced teacher and her mentee. "It's like an egg!" Mary, the seasoned teacher, said with a twinkle in her eye as she started to explain some of the basics of teaching to Rita, her mentee. The puzzled look on Rita's face evoked the need for further explanation. "Like an egg," continued Mary, "our mission as teachers is packed with potential for new life, nutritional energy, and unique structure. A lot of what we do starts deep inside, out of sight, like the yoke that represents relationships with ourselves and with others: This is where life begins. The protein in the egg white provides the strength and energy new life needs to grow—much like relevance helps us make sense of all that is around us. The shell provides the structure and protection we need, like the rigor of excellence to make sure we are safe." Rita listened intently and reflected how everything she does in the teaching-learning interaction is much like growing new life in a protected environment.

Preservice teachers benefit from the mentoring of experienced teachers who are willing to share their wisdom. Experienced teachers who are constantly in the process of professional growth benefit from collaboration with colleagues who are willing to pursue creative ways to develop learning classrooms. Teachers who keep learning are the best at teaching learning. Chart 7.1 contrasts professional growth among teachers from a learning classroom with professional growth among teachers from a managed classroom.

"Teachers who keep learning are the best at teaching learning."

—*Nic Cooper*

Chart 7.1   Professional Growth Among Teachers From a Learning Classroom vs. a Managed Classroom

Professional Growth With Teachers From a Learning Classroom	Professional Growth With Teachers From a Managed Classroom
Relationships with colleagues build community of professional learners to support classroom learning.	Relationships with colleagues is limited to required meetings; collaboration is resisted.
Relevance is pursued by teachers through ongoing professional development and inviting students to make connections with their world.	Relevance is low priority; teachers only focus on what they think is important; professional development is waste of time.
Rigor involves personal integrity and self-discipline for students and teacher.	Rigor involves teacher enforcing rules for students.
Positive school culture is cooperative, encouraging, and supportive.	Negative school culture is competitive, isolated, cynical, and critical.
Conversations are reflective and connected.	Conversations are defensive and argumentative.
Teachers are comfortable leading.	Teachers resist leadership positions.
Decisions are made based on the impact on learning and how they can be sustained.	Decisions are made without input and based on reaction to economic and political pressures.
The past is valued and used as a learning experience.	The past is revered and seen as the focus for the future.
Creative solutions to problems are encouraged and solicited.	Creativity is shunned; status quo is maintained.

REFLECTION

After reading this chapter, take a few minutes to reflect on the following:

- Examine the processes for determining professional development in your school system. Do these processes facilitate fluid change and adaptations? Are teachers invited to lead and provide meaningful input?
- Reflect on your openness to change. What factors influence your willingness to get involved? How have you overcome these obstacles?
- Reflect on your purpose in life and your profession. How are you fulfilling your purpose? To what extent do your thoughts and actions support your purpose?

- Reflect on what feeds your passion. What excites you about teaching? What frustrates or steals your passion?
- Under what conditions do you feel your persistence challenged? What do you do about it? Why is persistence important to you?

ACTION

- Identify other teachers who share your ideas and interests. Begin a book study using this book.
- Identify a school that is exceptional. Visit or interview the staff and observe how it operates. Blue ribbon schools or Schools to Watch would be good ones to notice. Examine how they feel and how they are organized. Journal about what you notice.
- Identify someone whom you see as being resistant to change. Initiate a conversation with this person with the goal of learning about him or her. Stay focused on learning that person's perspective and the background that led to it. Journal about the experience after you have the conversation.
- Have a similar conversation with someone who appears to embrace change. Journal about that experience also.
- Use the action research model to do a mini research project. Select a burning question or issue that puzzles you. Be sure to focus on your own practice and how you can collect and analyze data to improve your teaching.

Appendix A

Introductory Student Survey
(Also Available at http://www.corwin.com/books/Book237330)

(Print Name)_____ Date_____ Grade/Subject_____

What are you good at?

What do you wish you were good at?

What do you wish was easier in school?

What activities are you involved in outside of school?

What two words would you use to describe yourself?

How do you like to spend your free time?

What kind of things do you like to read?

What are your favorite TV programs? Movies? Music?

What are your favorite video games?

What do you want to be (do) when you "grow up"? Why?

What do you want your teacher to know about you?

Appendix B

Advanced Student Survey
(Also Available at http://www.corwin.com/books/
Book237330)

(Print Name)_____ Date_____ Grade/Subject_____

1. What do you wish the teacher would stop doing?

2. What do you wish the teacher would do more?

3. What do you wish you were good at?

4. What kind of things do you like to do at school?

5. What kind of things do you like to do outside of school?

6. What do you like best about yourself?

7. How do you go about figuring things out when you are stuck?

8. Whom do you admire the most and would love to be like? Why?

9. If you had the power and resources to change something, what would it be?

10. If you had three wishes, what would they be?

11. What do you wish you could change about the past? Why?

12. When you dream about the future, what do you see?

13. If I were a new student in your class, what would the other kids tell me about you?

14. What do you wish others knew about you?

15. What three things do you say to yourself most often?

Appendix C

Sample Socratic Questions: Tools to Stimulate Critical Thinking

The overall purpose of questioning is to enhance understanding.

CONCEPTUAL CLARIFICATION: BASIC "TELL ME MORE" QUESTIONS TO GO DEEPER

- *Help me understand what you mean by . . . ? Give me an example.*
- *What essential things do we need to know about this?*
- *How can you say that another way?*

PROBING ASSUMPTIONS: UNDERLYING BIASES, ASSUMPTIONS, BELIEFS, AND VALUES

- *What do you believe about this issue?*
- *Why is this important or relevant to you?*
- *What basic assumptions are involved here?*
- *What would happen if . . . ?*

PROBING RATIONALE, REASONS, AND EVIDENCE: BASIC PRINCIPLES AND MOTIVATION

- *Why did you choose this?*
- *What evidence do you base this on?*
- *What causes this to happen?*
- *How can you support your position?*
- *Why? (Ask about six times after each response.)*

QUESTIONING VIEWPOINTS AND PERSPECTIVES (DIFFERENT WAYS OF LOOKING)

- *What are alternative ways of looking at this?*
- *What is the difference between . . . and . . . ? How are they alike?*
- *What are the strengths and weaknesses of . . . ?*
- *How are . . . and . . . similar?*

PROBING IMPLICATIONS AND CONSEQUENCES

- *What will happen next? Why?*
- *Who will be affected by this?*
- *How could . . . be used to . . . ?*
- *What are the implications of . . . ?*
    - → *Beware of leading questions* that influence responder to desired answer.
    - → *Avoid close-ended questions* that can be answered with yes/no or a single word.
    - → *Use open-ended questions* that encourage reflection without fear of being wrong.
    - → Use the wh-questions:
        - ○ *What* identifies specific details related to an issue.
        - ○ *Why* identifies reasoning and logical connections of an issue.
        - ○ *When* identifies elements of time such as duration or specific moment.
        - ○ *Where* identifies location in space.
        - ○ *Who* identifes persons involved.
        - ○ *How* identifies process of doing something.

For more information, see http://changingminds.org/techniques/questioning/socratic_questions.htm.

Appendix D

Flexible Lesson Design

Teacher selects content and designs instructional goals and activities.

1. Students experience and explore (*sensory input* and *cognitive engagement*):
   - Provide concrete materials for students to touch, see, hear, smell, taste, and interact with. Instead of telling the students what something is like, provide experiences so that they can tell teacher and each other what they notice.
   - Encourage students to *notice things* and share their curiosity and observations. Students need to "see with their eyes"—the physical characteristics of objects. Students also need to "see with their minds"—the connections and unusual things they notice and have questions about. (*How the teacher relates to the students and interacts with them affects how engaged the students will be in the activity.*)

2. Students share (bring something to the learning; use cognitive processing):
   - Provide time for students to describe and discuss with each other what they noticed and wondered about.
   - Encourage students to ask questions. (*How the teacher reacts to students' questions determines whether or not the students will feel comfortable to ask questions.*)

3. Teacher introduces new materials and concepts (*expanded processing*):
   - Provide connections between student experience and feedback and new information being presented. Pace content and skills so that students can enjoy the challenge of new learning and the satisfaction of understanding.

○ Encourage cognitive, physical, and emotional engagement. Present material in multiple ways to meet needs of individual students. (*Teacher competence, enthusiasm, relationship with students, organization, and ability to make information relevant directly affect students' willingness to learn new material.*)

4. Students give evidence of learning (*output through synthesis* and *application*):
   ○ Provide time, coaching, and materials for students to demonstrate their understanding of the new concepts. (*Teacher's willingness to look for, validate, and build on the students' strengths and let students do the work greatly enhances students' learning.*)
   ○ Encourage continued questioning and learning through research projects (group and individual) related to the new information.
   ○ Encourage application of new information to life through relevant action to influence change (write letters, fax, call, send e-mail, research Internet, interview, etc.).
   ○ Encourage creative ways to demonstrate understanding:
      ◆ In writing (written report, journal, letters, editorials)
      ◆ Orally (verbal report, role playing, drama, newscast format, power point, music)
      ◆ Graphically (video, drawing, posters, painting, construction of models)
      ◆ By teaching information to someone else or making up an assessment
      ◆ By using digital formats and multimedia presentations

5. Students and teachers reflect (*evaluation of learning experience*):
   ○ Provide opportunity to reflectively respond to question: "What sense did I make of this?"
   ○ Encourage students to help develop scoring guides to evaluate effectiveness of learning. (*How teachers and students collaborate to evaluate learning determines personal investment in continued learning.*)
   ○ Discuss with students: What could we do differently to improve this learning experience?
   ○ Develop plan of action: What will students do as a result of this learning? How will they continue to use it in everyday life and other subject areas?

Appendix E

Personal Education Plan
(Also Available at http://www.corwin.com/books/
Book237330)

The personal education plan can be transferred to any easily handled system from electronic to a three-ring binder and note cards. The idea is to focus on getting to know students on a deeper level by seeking to understand them from different perspectives. Lengthy narratives are not necessary. Instead, brief understandable notes that can inform instructional decisions for this student are best to make the task realistic and helpful.

(Print Name)_____ Date_____ Grade/Subject_____

Interests: (List the interests that the student volunteers or that you notice from observing and listening.)

Learning profile: (How does this student learn best? Be sure to get the student's ideas on this as well as what you might notice.)

Skills: (What skills does the student exhibit or talk about? Also notice those that are not school related. These might provide ideas on how to make this student feel capable.)

Growth areas: (In what ways does this student need to grow? Think in terms of intellectual, emotional, and social growth.)

Cultural considerations: (Are there cultural considerations to be understood? These might include ethnic considerations, as well as economic, but also regional.)

Family considerations: (Are there special family issues that concern you or that will help support this student?)

Behavioral issues: (What misbehavior arises? What might be the cause?)

Interventions: (What interventions have you used? Which ones worked? Which ones didn't?)

School connections: (What friends or adults are connected to this student in school?)

Community connections: (What groups in the community support this student?)

Other: (What else do you notice about this student?)

References

Alberta's Teachers' Association. (May, 2011). *The impact of digital technologies on teachers working in flexible learning environments.* Retrieved from http://www.teachers.ab.ca/SiteCollectionDocuments/ATA/Publications/Research-Updates/PD-86-21%20Impact%20of%20Digital%20Technologies.pdf

Anderson, L.W., & Krathwohl, D. R. (Eds.). (2000). *A taxonomy for learning, teaching, and assessing: A revision of Bloom's taxonomy of educational objectives* (2nd ed.). New York, NY: Pearson.

Cooper, N., & McCoy, R. (1999). *How to keep being a parent when your child stops being a child: A practical guide to parenting adolescents.* Canton, MI: Willow Creek.

Csikszentmihalyi, M. (2008). *Flow: The psychology of optimal experience.* New York, NY: Harper Perennial Modern Classics.

Cunningham, W. G., & Gresso, D. W. (1993). *Cultural leadership: The culture of excellence in education.* Boston, MA: Allyn & Bacon.

Duckworth, E. R. (2005). Critical exploration in the classroom. *New Educator, 1*(4), 257–272.

Duckworth, E. R. (2006). *The having of wonderful ideas.* New York, NY: Teachers College, Columbia University.

Dweck, C. S. (2006). *Mindset: The new psychology of success.* New York, NY: Random House.

Fortin, D. A., Srivastava, T., & Soderling, T. R. (2011, June 13). Structural modulation of dendritic spines during synaptic plasticity [Epub]. *Neuroscientist.* Retrieved from http://www.ncbi.nlm.nih.gov/pubmed/21670426

Garmston, R. J., & Wellman, B. M. (2009). *Adaptive schools: A sourcebook for developing collaborative groups* (2nd ed.). Norwood, MA: Christopher-Gordon.

Garner, B. K. (2007). *Getting to "Got It!": Helping struggling students learn how to learn.* Alexandria, VA: ASCD.

Haffar, A. (2009, July 29). *Critical thinking through learner-centered teaching: An interview with Eleanor Duckworth, Professor at Harvard Graduate School of Education.* Retrieved from http://www.modernghana.com/news2/229750/1/critical-thinking-through-learner-centred-teaching.html

Hoerr, T. R. (2012, December/January). What are parents thinking? *Educational Leadership, 69*(4), 90–91.

Jackson, R. R. (2009). *Never work harder than your students and other principles of great teaching.* Alexandria, VA: ASCD.

Jackson, R. R. (2011). *How to plan rigorous instruction.* Alexandria, VA: ASCD.

Jacobs, H. H. (Ed.). (2010). *Curriculum 21: Essential education for a changing world.* Alexandria, VA: ASCD.

Jensen, E. (2011). The special needs brain. In D. A. Sousa (Ed.), *Best of Corwin: Educational neuroscience* (pp. 127–138).Thousand Oaks, CA: Corwin.

Kagan, S., & Kagan, M. (2009). *Kagan cooperative learning*. Kagan: San Clemente, CA. Retrieved from www.kaganonline.com

Marzano, R. J. (2012, December/January). It's how you use a strategy. *Educational Leadership, 69*(4), 88–89.

Marzano, R. J., Frontier, R. J., & Livingston, D. (2011). *Effective supervision: supporting the art and science of teaching*. Alexandria, VA: ASCD.

Tomlinson, C. A. (2012, December/January). The chance to test our mettle. *Educational Leadership, 69*(4), 92–93.

Tovani, C. (2011). *So what do they really know? Assessment that informs teaching and learning*. Portland, ME: Stenhouse.

United Nations Educational, Scientific and Cultural Organization. (2001, November 2). UNESCO Universal Declaration on Cultural Diversity. Retrieved from http://portal.unesco.org/en/ev.php-URL_ID=13179&URL_DO=DO_TOPIC&URL_SECTION=201.html

Wiggins, G. (2011, April). Moving to modern assessments. *Phi Delta Kappan, 92*(7), 63.

Willis, J. (2006). *Research-based strategies to ignite student learning: Insight from a neurologist and classroom teacher*. Alexandria, VA: ASCD.

Wong, H. K., & Wong, R. T. (2009). *The first days of school: How to be an effective teacher* (4th rev. ed.). Mountain View, CA: Harry K. Wong.

Index

CORWIN

A SAGE Company

The Corwin logo—a raven striding across an open book—represents the union of courage and learning. Corwin is committed to improving education for all learners by publishing books and other professional development resources for those serving the field of PreK–12 education. By providing practical, hands-on materials, Corwin continues to carry out the promise of its motto: **"Helping Educators Do Their Work Better."**